teach® yourself

ietzsche

nietzsche

roy jackson

For UK order enquiries: please contact Bookpoint Ltd, 130 Milton Park, Abingdon, Oxon, OX14 4SB. Telephone: +44 (0) 1235 827720. Fax: +44 (0) 1235 400454. Lines are open from 09.00–17.00, Monday to Saturday, with a 24-hour message answering service. Details about our titles and how to order are available at www.teachyourself.co.uk

For USA order enquiries: please contact McGraw-Hill Customer Services, PO Box 545, Blacklick, OH 43004-0545, USA. Telephone: 1-800-722-4726. Fax: 1-614-755-5645.

For Canada order enquiries: please contact McGraw-Hill Ryerson Ltd, 300 Water St, Whitby, Ontario, L1N 9B6, Canada. Telephone: 905 430 5000. Fax: 905 430 5020.

Long renowned as the authoritative source for self-guided learning – with more than 50 million copies sold worldwide – the **teach yourself** series includes over 500 titles in the fields of languages, crafts, hobbies, business, computing and education.

British Library Cataloguing in Publication Data: a catalogue record for this title is available from the British Library.

Library of Congress Catalog Card Number: on file.

First published in UK 2008 by Hodder Education, part of Hachette Livre UK, 338 Euston Road, London, NW1 3BH.

First published in US 2008 by The McGraw-Hill Companies, Inc.

This edition published 2008.

The **teach yourself** name is a registered trademark of Hodder Headline.

Copyright © 2008 Roy Jackson

Typeset by Transet Limited, Coventry, England.
Printed in Great Britain for Hodder Education, an Hachette Livre UK Company, 338 Euston Road, London, NW1 3BH, by CPI Cox & Wyman Ltd, Reading, Berkshire, RG1 8EX.

The publisher has used its best endeavours to ensure that the URLs for external websites referred to in this book are correct and active at the time of going to press. However, the publisher and the author have no responsibility for the websites and can make no guarantee that a site will remain live or that the content will remain relevant, decent or appropriate.

Hachette Livre UK's policy is to use papers that are natural, renewable and recyclable products and made from wood grown in sustainable forests. The logging and manufacturing processes are expected to conform to the environmental regulations of the country of origin.

Impression number   10 9 8 7 6 5 4 3 2 1
Year   2012 2011 2010 2009 2008

contents

dedication		ix
introduction		xi
	a time of change	xii
	reading Nietzsche	xiii
	on interpreting Nietzsche	xvii
	summary	xviii
01	**Nietzsche's early life 1844–79**	**1**
	Nietzsche's background	2
	tragedy strikes	3
	Nietzsche's education	5
	the professor	6
	the influence of Wagner	9
	the Bayreuth Festival of 1876	12
	the influence of Schopenhauer	14
	summary	20
02	**Nietzsche's later life and death 1879–1900**	**21**
	Malwida von Meysenbug (1816–1903) and Paul Rée (1849–1901)	22
	Nietzsche's 'wanderings'	24
	Lou von Salomé (1861–1937)	28
	the final years	31
	the Nietzsche Archive	34
	summary	35
03	***The Birth of Tragedy***	**37**
	the 'theoretical man'	39
	Apollo and Dionysus	42

		the importance of culture	45
		the value of Greek tragedy	48
		summary	51
	04	**the revaluation of all values**	**53**
		morality	54
		the death of God	55
		Nietzsche's naturalism	56
		slave morality	61
		ressentiment	63
		the priests	66
		the revaluation of all values	67
		summary	69
	05	**the will to power**	**71**
		what is the will to power?	72
		the enigma of the will to power	72
		first interpretation: an objective explanation for everything	75
		second interpretation: a subjective interpretation	79
		a third interpretation: the will to power as empirically true	83
		concluding remarks	86
		summary	87
	06	**Zarathustra, the Superman and the eternal recurrence**	**89**
		Thus Spoke Zarathustra	90
		a brief summary of Thus Spoke Zarathustra	91
		the eternal recurrence	94
		the Superman	98
		after Zarathustra	100
		nihilism	100
		amor fati	103
		the need for consolation	104
		summary	105
	07	**on truth and perspectivism**	**107**
		varieties of truth	108
		Nietzsche's perspectivism	110
		reason and the senses	113

	the importance of language	114
	summary	117
08	**Nietzsche and religion**	**119**
	Nietzsche's religiosity	120
	Nietzsche as a 'sort' of atheist	121
	Nietzsche the Lutheran	122
	Nietzsche and 'inspiration'	123
	religion as life-enhancing	124
	on Islam	125
	myth, modernity and monumental history	127
	religion and the state	129
	on Buddhism	132
	summary	133
09	**Nietzsche and politics**	**135**
	democracy	136
	the immoralist?	141
	on women	143
	the philosophers of the future	146
	does Nietzsche have any political views?	147
	summary	149
10	**Nietzsche's legacy**	**151**
	Nazism	152
	twentieth-century French philosophy	155
	the analytic tradition	159
	art	160
	other influences	161
	summary	162
glossary		**163**
taking it further		**167**
	timeline of important events in Nietzsche's life	**167**
	chronology of major works	**168**
	further reading	**169**
	websites	**170**
index		**171**

dedication

To Raef and Nadiya

introduction

Friedrich Nietzsche was a German philosopher. He lived from 1844 to 1900 and is most famous for his declaration that 'God is dead' and his consequent belief that we must therefore create a new man, a 'Superman'. Nietzsche is probably the most widely-read philosopher in the modern world, yet he also continues to be the most misunderstood. His writings were almost totally ignored during his lifetime and, up until the mid-twentieth century, his philosophy was neglected and badly translated. Up until then his influence has been claimed in areas as diverse as vegetarianism, anarchism, Nazism and religious cultism. It is only more recently that Nietzsche has undergone something of a rehabilitation and a deserved recognition has emerged that here was a man who ranks amongst the great and original thinkers of the modern age.

Nietzsche was the first philosopher to fully confront the prevailing loss of religious belief in Western Europe with his declaration that 'God is dead'. What Nietzsche meant by this was that society no longer had a need for God for He had outlived his usefulness. Nietzsche was therefore calling for humanity to stand on its own two feet without the support of faith or dogma of any kind. Nietzsche, therefore, was not only attacking religious faith, but also a belief in objective values or truths. We must *choose our own values*. The reason people persisted in a belief in God or truth, Nietzsche argued, was because of their reluctance to face the reality of the situation; it is a form of self-deception. Rather it is better to face and, indeed, to embrace, the temporary nature of existence and the apparent meaninglessness of life.

Nietzsche suffered from severe illness throughout much of his life, including severe migraines which meant he often lay in a darkened room, unable to leave his bed. He went insane in January 1889, and his illness and insanity may well be the result of contracting syphilis, although he suffered from headaches even as a boy. Nietzsche, however, saw illness in a positive way, providing him with the inspiration to write and think: great works come from suffering, he believed. Indeed, he was able to write his greatest works during perhaps the times of his worse suffering, both physically and mentally. Works such as *Thus Spoke Zarathustra*, *Beyond Good and Evil*, and *Genealogy of Morals* were all written between 1883 and 1887.

A time of change

Nietzsche was born at a time of great change. The age of the telegraph had arrived in the year of Nietzsche's birth, Karl Marx's *Communist Manifesto* was published when Nietzsche was four and, in the same year, revolutions were breaking out across Europe with the growth in new values and ideas such as popular liberalism, nationalism and socialism. Over the next two decades, Germany (under Bismarck) and Italy achieved political unification, Austria and Prussia eliminated feudalism and, in 1861, Russia freed the serfs. From the 1870s the second phase of the Industrial Revolution led to mass production of goods and the mechanization of society. Importantly, from a religious perspective, belief in God was on the decline: Marx had declared it to be the opium of the masses and Charles Darwin's (1809–82) theory of evolution raised serious religious questions regarding the authority of the Bible. Nietzsche was to present a critical eye over these changes: of the dangers of Enlightenment ideals, of increasing mechanization and secularization, of democracy and liberalism and of nihilism. In many respects, Nietzsche can be seen as a prophet of his time, yet also out of step with his time, as prophets often are. Whilst many head like lemmings towards the cliff edge, singing the praises of science and political enlightenment, Nietzsche stands upon the top of a high

mountain and looks down from another perspective, one of
caution and warning of the possible dangers of this new age.

He is certainly the most controversial and notorious philosopher
to have lived, as well as being one of the world's most interesting
and scintillating you will come across in the realms of philosophy
at least. When people think of Nietzsche today they associate
him with his harsh criticisms of religion, specifically Christianity,
as well as his attack on the belief in 'another world'. Previous to
his rehabilitation, however, many did not regard him as much of
a philosopher at all but, even worse, someone who should be
banned from the bookshelves. The reasons for this perception of
Nietzsche will be unravelled as you read on, and even the current
understanding of him can be considered as open to debate. The
fact that today you can attend Nietzsche conferences were he is
discussed amongst serious and highly professional philosophers
should be sufficient evidence that here we are talking about
Nietzsche as a very serious philosopher indeed.

Reading Nietzsche

The best way to get to know Nietzsche is to read him for
yourself. His unusual style and lyrical approach to philosophy
can, for the reader coming to the philosopher for the first time,
be both unnerving and confusing, especially if that reader is used
to the more conventional linear and discursive approach to
argument. Even Nietzsche's mature and most coherent work can
still leave the student searching for thematic hooks from which
to hang the philosopher's cloak. One renowned scholar of
Nietzsche, Michael Tanner, remarked upon what is perhaps
Nietzsche's best book, *Beyond Good and Evil*:

> If one goes through the text of *Beyond Good and Evil*
> using a high-lighter, one's likely to find that one has
> marked more than half the book. It comes as a shock
> when one re-reads it a month later, say, and finds not only
> that one is reading many of the high-lighted passages as if
> for the first time, but that one is scandalized by one's non-

high-lighting of other wonderful passages, and occasionally bewildered at what one did mark.

However, not only does Nietzsche present unambiguous themes in this text but also, with patience and perseverance, it can be seen that Nietzsche writes in a lucid and logical manner. When reading commentaries on Nietzsche the reader must be aware that only relatively recently has he experienced a deserved rehabilitation. You will not have to dip very far into the past to read works by scholars that rely upon poor translations of Nietzsche's work, or take his published notes (not published by Nietzsche himself, but his anti-Semitic sister Elisabeth) as evidence of his final philosophy.

Nietzsche's works do not, on the whole, lend themselves to a straightforward understanding; using, as he does, metaphor, symbol, irony, sarcasm, and 'in jokes'. This is certainly part of his attraction for readers, but also helps explain why his works were condemned by the academic community for their lack of academic rigour, detailed research, compartmentalization or high standards of source evidence.

If you take the time to read some of Nietzsche's works chronologically, you will see how he gradually develops his own voice; breaking away from the influence of the composer Richard Wagner and the philosopher Arthur Schopenhauer, and developing a distinctive writing style that, though hard-hitting and poetic, was not regarded as the correct form to use for works of good philosophy. Nietzsche started writing in aphorisms: catchy passages varying in length from a single sentence to a short essay of several pages. This style may well be a result of Nietzsche's long walks in the mountains when he would stop at various points and jot down some idea or other. Whatever the reason, Nietzsche developed an undeserved reputation for writing in a jumbled and ill-considered fashion. In fact, Nietzsche always thought long and hard about the structure of his books which, more recently, has caused analogies to be made between his writings and the sonata form in music. In fact, Nietzsche did also compose some music.

Yet aphorisms are a hazardous form of writing. A good aphorism strikes the reader as brilliant and memorable, whereas a bad aphorism will be quickly forgotten. Fortunately, Nietzsche was, on the whole, a brilliant aphorist. Yet the reader has to approach an aphorism differently from linear, discursive argument. Whereas the latter, if it is any good, flows along in a gradual manner, revealing its premises one by one, each aphorism, on the other hand, has to be treated as both self-contained and yet part of a greater whole. There are times when Nietzsche seems to slip in an aphorism that leaves the reader pondering over its relevance and it may be some time later in the book before that relevance becomes clear if, that is, the reader can remember having read it! Aphorisms share a number of features with poetry, especially in their intention of engaging the reader on a personal level and requiring you to agree and be affected by what they are attempting to illuminate. Like good poetry, an aphorism can be enlightening and life-changing. As Nietzsche comments in his work *Ecce Homo*, he writes so that his reader can dip into his books as if they were jumping into a glacial stream, that is, in and out quickly with the expectation that the experience will be remembered for some time to come.

However, because aphorisms are not simply intended to inform, describe and present a thesis, it is difficult for the student especially (as opposed to the casual reader) to know what is relevant, to know – referring to Michael Tanner's quote above – what to highlight. How can you argue with an aphorism? In *Thus Spoke Zarathustra*, Nietzsche says, 'Whoever writes in blood and aphorisms wants not to be read but to be learned by heart.' Nietzsche, something of a child prodigy, was educated at a public school, Pforta. No doubt he would have had to commit many works, classics especially, to memory. The advantage of this kind of study may not be immediately obvious, but those who still operate in this way argue that it pays in the future when the relevance can be seen. However, unless you intend for Nietzsche to become your guide for life, it can hardly be expected for the student to learn Nietzsche's aphorisms by heart, and nor would it be particularly beneficial in understanding in the more immediate term. A more pragmatic approach needs to be adopted.

In reading Nietzsche it is difficult to find the 'real Nietzsche': that is, to find the answer to the question, what did Nietzsche *really* think? But if someone were to ask you what *you* really think, how sincerely could you answer that question? We all have a collection of thoughts and some are more certain than others, yet we also change our attitude and beliefs about things over time as we learn more. Nietzsche, like so many philosophers before and after him, is no exception to this. There seems to be a view by some that those 'in authority' cannot change their minds, but it could be said that the real thinker is someone who is open-minded enough to acknowledge that views can change. As you read Nietzsche you will see that there are certain key topics that he keeps coming back to with new insights, amendments and better arguments. His views do change over time and, as such, his writings must be seen as a process, as thinking things through. This can prove to be very frustrating for the interpreter, but can also be something of an intellectual joy.

Another point to keep in mind when reading *this* book is that it is simply not possible to cover all aspects of Nietzsche's philosophy. His writings are wide-ranging indeed, covering such traditional topics as moral philosophy, politics, aesthetics (theory of art), epistemology (theory of knowledge) and religion. However, he also talks about history, women, food, sex, the self, mysticism, and so on in an often bizarre and controversial manner that can leave the reader questioning the writer's grip on reality. On that point, although he did have a mental breakdown in 1889 from which he was never to recover, there is no reason to suppose that any of his writing previous to this is the product of an insane man: a genius and unconventional thinker, yes, but a madman, no. Having said that, as Nietzsche would readily admit, the line between madness and genius is very thin indeed.

On interpreting Nietzsche

If you get more involved in Nietzsche, perhaps studying him at university, doing some independent research, or attending conferences, you will note that over the past 30 years or so two very distinct interpretive schools of philosophical interpretation of Nietzsche have developed with differing approaches to studying his work. First there is the *continental* approach, which was dominant in French philosophy especially from the 1960s onwards and has been championed by such philosophical greats as Michel Foucault, Gilles Deleuze and Jacques Derrida (see Chapter 09). The continental tradition, though something of a gross generalization to say this, concentrates more on Nietzsche's style: his playful and clever use of language, his poetic and imaginative use of metaphor and humour, and so on. This is not to say that content is not important, but that the content has to be understood within the context of Nietzsche's play on words and his use of the German language. The continental tradition has generally defended Nietzsche as someone who is something of an existentialist who argues for no objective moral values and knowledge as a matter of perspective.

Again, though something of a generalization, the continental tradition sees Nietzsche as more radical and ahead of his time than that of the other philosophical school, the *analytic* tradition, would have him. Analytic philosophy is a multi-faceted phenomenon, but essentially what characterizes it from other traditions in philosophy is that it tends to align itself closely with the sciences and to focus on clarification of terms rather than produce whole systems of philosophy which was more common in the European tradition. In this sense, analytic philosophy may seem less 'ambitious' but, at the same time, perhaps more realistic in achieving targets. Analytic philosophers – who are largely part of the Anglo-American world – see Nietzsche in a more traditional sense rather than as a radical existentialist figure.

In this work it is hoped that both these traditions are given due worth, but ultimately such distinctions should not matter. The fact remains that Nietzsche has something to say, whether you are an adherent of a particular philosophical school or just someone who enjoys a good read.

Summary

- Nietzsche was a German philosopher whose most famous declaration was 'God is dead'. In this, he was the first philosopher to fully confront the prevailing loss of religious belief in Western Europe.
- Nietzsche was alive during a period of great change and his writings reflect his concerns over this.
- Reading Nietzsche is difficult, given his unique style.
- Nietzsche is interpreted in many ways, primarily in the philosophical traditions it is divided into two schools: the continental and the analytic.

Nietzsche's texts – Abbreviations

Ecce Homo: **EH**
Thus Spoke Zarathustra: **TSZ**
Birth of Tragedy: **BT**
Beyond Good and Evil: **BGE**
The Twilight of the Idols: **TI**
The Antichrist: **AC**
The Gay Science: **GS**
The Genealogy of Morals: **GM**
Untimely Meditations: **UM**
Human, All Too Human: **HAH.**

01

Nietzsche's early life 1844–79

In this chapter you will learn:

- about Nietzsche's family and background
- about his education at school and university
- about his teaching career
- about the influences of Wagner and Schopenhauer.

All in all I could not have endured my youth without Wagnerian music. For I was condemned to Germans. If one wants to get free from an unendurable pressure one needs hashish. Very well, I needed Wagner. Wagner is the counter-poison to everything German par excellence – still poison, I do not dispute it.

(*EH*, 'Why I Am So Clever')

Nietzsche's background

Nietzsche was born on 15 October 1844 in Röcken, which is a municipality in the district of Burgenlandkreis in Saxony-Anhalt in Germany. Even today Röcken is a small village with a population of less than 200. You can still see the house, the Pastor's house, where Nietzsche was born which has now become a museum. You can also visit the ancient church (one of the oldest in Saxony) where he was baptized, his village school, and the well-kept family grave where he is buried next to his sister Elisabeth and his parents. Röcken was surrounded by farms and the nearest town, Lützen, was a half-hour walk away and was itself a very small market town.

Nietzsche's ancestry has been traced back to the sixteenth century of some 200 German forebears. None were aristocrats and most were small tradesmen such as butchers and carpenters. However, he is also the heir of some 20 clergymen. Nietzsche's grandfather was a superintendent (the equivalent of a bishop) in the Lutheran Church, and the philosopher's father, Karl Ludwig, became pastor for the village. Friedrich's mother, Franziska Oehler, was the daughter of the Lutheran pastor of a neighbouring village. The first five-and-a-half years of Nietzsche's life were spent in a parsonage, and even after that he was brought up in a pious environment. It is curious to note that the philosopher who came to symbolize more than any other the rejection of religious dogma, was brought up within such an observant household. His philosophy has, as a result, been seen as a deliberate rebellion against a strict, oppressive and conformist upbringing. Yet the Lutheran Church resembles more the Anglican rather than some fundamentalist, puritan church. In fact, the Lutheran tradition has contributed greatly to German intellectual and cultural life and has encouraged cultural and social improvement. There is every indication that the young Friedrich had a happy and fulfilling childhood, and he never spoke in his writings of any kind of rebellion against his upbringing. If anything, the young Nietzsche was more strict and conformist than his peers.

Nietzsche's father was 30 years old when, in 1843, he married the 17-year-old Franziska. Nietzsche shared a birthday with the reigning King of Prussia and so was named Friedrich Wilhelm after him. After Friedrich, they gave birth to a daughter, Elisabeth, in 1846, and a second son, Joseph, in 1848. Also residing in the house were Nietzsche's two rather dotty aunts and Franziska's widowed mother. By all accounts, Nietzsche's mother possessed a great deal of common sense and unquestioning piety, but had not been well-educated. The first years of Nietzsche's life were quiet ones as the family settled down to their existence together. The descriptions of the house and its surrounds conjure up an idyllic setting with a small farmyard, an orchard, a flower garden and ponds surrounded by willow trees. Here Nietzsche could fish and play, exercising his imagination as all children do. According to his sister Elisabeth's memoirs, Nietzsche took up talking rather late to the extent that, at the age of two-and-a-half, his parents consulted a physician who suggested that the reason he hadn't spoken was because the family doted upon him so much he felt there was no need to talk. His first word, apparently, was 'Granma', an indication of the female influence in the household, and by the age of four he began to read and write.

Tragedy strikes

Although childhood was, on the whole, a happy one for Friedrich, in 1849 tragedy struck with the death of his father. Karl Ludwig was only 36. A year later, Nietzsche's younger brother also died. The traditional family existence was shattered and they were compelled to leave Röcken to go to the nearby walled town of Naumburg. The young Friedrich now lived with his mother, sister, two maiden aunts and a maternal grandmother. Women, therefore, surrounded Nietzsche, and his younger sister especially doted upon him. Nietzsche's mother was still very young, but she was never to remarry. Nietzsche was very close to his father and there has been much speculation over the psychological impact that his father's death, as well as the causes of his death, might have had upon the philosopher. There is little evidence to show why the Pastor died so young, other than he was the victim of minor epileptic fits and he died from some kind of brain affliction. The speculation that he suffered from insanity is not substantiated, but it was a belief for Nietzsche that diseases are hereditary and that he was therefore destined for a short life himself. In his later writings, Nietzsche often paints an idealistic picture of his father. Perhaps the most famous account is in his work *Ecce Homo* which Nietzsche wrote when he was 44 years of age:

> ... he was delicate, lovable and morbid, like a being destined to pay this world only a passing visit – a gracious reminder of life rather than life itself.

> (*EH* ii)

In many respects life at Naumburg would have differed little from Röcken, for it too was a small town that saw or cared little for the outside world. Nietzsche was to live there until he was 14. His mother, as a result of legacies left by her own mother on her death in 1856, had the financial means to set up a home of her own. Nietzsche attended the local boys' school where he made his earliest friends, Wilhelm Pinder and Gustav Krug. Pinder, at the age of 14, wrote an autobiography and makes regular mention of Nietzsche, describing his initial encounter with the young Friedrich as one of the most important events in his life. The picture Wilhelm presents of the boy Nietzsche is of someone who loved solitude and had a pious, tender temperament whilst having a lively, inventive and independent mind. Significantly his character is portrayed as someone who displayed the virtues of humility and gratitude and was preparing himself for a future vocation as a pastor. Pinder's father was a town councillor and lover of literature and used to read Goethe to the three boys. Krug's father was an amateur musician and we can detect Nietzsche's life-long love of music originating here as he took it upon himself to learn to play the piano.

Nietzsche's education

In 1851, the three boyhood friends were transferred from the town school to the private preparatory school until 1854. Here Nietzsche received his first taste of Latin and Greek. They all went on to the higher school, the *Domgymnasium*, until 1858 when Nietzsche – no doubt due to his intellectual talents – was awarded a free boarding place at the exclusive and strict Pforta school. Nietzsche was studious, certainly, but he enjoyed outdoor activities such as walking, swimming and skating and grew to be physically well-built. However, he suffered from illness throughout most of his life and it was during these years that the headaches began, possibly linked also to his short-sightedness and the large amount of reading and writing he did as a child.

Pforta School was disciplined and traditional. Pupils were awoken at 4 a.m., classes started at 6 a.m. and continued until 4 p.m. There were further classes in the evening. The school concentrated on classical education – especially Latin and Greek – rather than mathematics and the sciences. Nietzsche developed an enthusiasm for poetry, literature and music, as well as scholarly criticism, which led him to doubt the tenets of the Bible.

When he went to the University of Bonn in 1864 to study philology (the study of language and literature) and theology he had already ceased to believe in the existence of God. At the university, Nietzsche soon abandoned the study of theology altogether, a subject which he had probably only agreed to do because of his mother's eagerness for him to become a pastor. Nietzsche never really settled down in Bonn and decided to go to Leipzig University in 1865 where he became much more studious.

During the Leipzig years (1865–9) there were a series of life-changing encounters. First of all, it was during this period that Nietzsche quite likely contracted syphilis by attending a brothel. Syphilis was incurable and could result in a life of periodic illness leading to insanity and early death. Secondly, while wandering around a second-hand bookshop, Nietzsche came across *The World as Will and Idea* (1819) by the German philosopher Arthur Schopenhauer (1788–1860). Nietzsche became a 'Schopenhauerian'. Schopenhauer's pessimistic view that the world is supported by an all-pervasive will that pays no attention to the concerns of humanity, fitted well with Nietzsche's feelings at the time. He also read the *History of Materialism* (1867) by the philosopher and social scientist F. A. Lange (1828–75) which introduced Nietzsche to Darwinian theories. And thirdly, on 28 October 1868, Nietzsche announced his conversion to the hugely influential composer and musical theorist Richard Wagner (1813–83) after hearing a performance of the *Tristan* and *Meistersinger* preludes. Only 11 days later he met Wagner in person. During that brief meeting, in which Wagner turned on the charm and entertained on the piano, Nietzsche discovered Wagner was also a Schopenhauerian. Wagner was born the same year as Nietzsche's father and bore some resemblance to him, and so developed into a father figure for Nietzsche.

Nietzsche's university professor considered him to be the finest student he had seen in 40 years. Consequently, Nietzsche was awarded his doctorate without examination and was recommended for a chair in classical philology at Basel University in 1869. At the age of 24, Nietzsche was already a university professor.

The professor

Between the ages of six and 34 – a total of 28 years – Nietzsche was never to leave the environs of the classroom for more than a few months during the holiday periods. This was, therefore, a period of intense and cloistered learning and it is perhaps no wonder that Nietzsche was to reject a career in academia. For the next ten years at Basel University, Nietzsche became less interested in philology and more enthusiastic towards philosophy. For Nietzsche, however, philosophy was not to be found by being immersed in books – which, essentially, was all that philology was concerned with – and he longed to expand his horizons. However, the lure of a salary and being able to support his mother was an important inducement in keeping the post.

Basel was essentially a German town, although it rested within Switzerland. In taking the post, Basel asked that he become a Swiss national so that he would not be called up for Prussian military service at any time that would interfere with his work. Nietzsche ceased to be a citizen of Prussia, but never succeeded in satisfying the residential requirements for Swiss citizenship. From 1869 onwards, Nietzsche remained stateless. Nonetheless, this did not prevent him from applying to be a nursing orderly for the Prussian forces during the Franco-Prussian War. It is quite possible that Nietzsche saw this as his opportunity to escape from the world of books, at least for a while. However, he suffered from diphtheria and ended up being nursed rather than being the nurse. After which, he returned to his teaching.

Despite his reservations, Nietzsche proved to be an able and popular teacher. Students spoke of his enthusiasm and their sense that this man had been transported through time from Ancient Greece; such was his knowledge and explication of the subject. A famous incident in class was when he suggested that the students read the account of Achilles' shield in Homer's *Iliad* over the summer vacation. At the beginning of the next term, Nietzsche asked a student to describe Achilles' shield to him. The embarrassed student had not read it, however, and there followed ten minutes of silence during which Nietzsche paced up and down and appeared to be listening attentively. After the time had elapsed, Nietzsche thanked the student for the description and moved on!

Nietzsche also developed his own physical appearance. By most accounts he was a smart dresser, almost to the extent of being something of a dandy. He began to cultivate his famous moustache that, in a famous photo of 1882, covered the whole of his mouth. There is another photo of Nietzsche with his mother taken in 1890, which shows the moustache reaching down to his chin!

At Basel University, Nietzsche developed a strong affection towards Jakob Burckhardt (1818–97), professor of the history of art and civilization. Burckhardt's greatest work, *The Civilisation of the Renaissance in Italy* (1860) continues to be important to this day. In it, Burckhardt outlined the historical transition from the Middle Ages to the Renaissance as a transformation from people who perceived themselves as belonging to a community to the idea of self-conscious individualism. When Nietzsche met him, Burckhardt had already been teaching at Basel for 26 years (and was to continue teaching there for another 24) and, although Nietzsche was in awe of this man, Burckhardt preferred a polite distance. Nietzsche's primary father figure, Wagner, however, now lived only 40 miles away in his villa called Tribschen on the shores of Lake Lucerne. In no time, Nietzsche became a regular weekend visitor there.

From 1871, Nietzsche started to become seriously ill: an illness that was to dog the rest of his life. While he had suffered from headaches since he was a child, now they were mostly in the form of severe migraine; so relentless that he could not eat and would have to remain in bed in a darkened room for days on end. These recurrent illnesses always left him exhausted, and so it is all the more amazing that he was able to work so prolifically. During an absence from university due to illness he worked on his first book, *The Birth of Tragedy* (1871). Although loved by Wagnerians, as it sung the praises of the composer, it was attacked by academics as little more than Wagnerian propaganda and lacking in scholarly study.

Nietzsche's illnesses became steadily worse, forcing him to spend less time at the university. He was also becoming disillusioned with Wagner, who he began to see as a sham philosopher. Also, Wagner had moved to Bayreuth, which put an end to the weekend visits. In 1878, Nietzsche wrote *Human, All Too Human*, a quite definitely anti-Wagnerian work which caused Wagner to say that Nietzsche would one day thank him for not reading it. This work, though stylistically a great improvement on *The Birth of Tragedy*, was still viewed as lacking in intellectual rigour or coherency. This, together with increased bouts of severe illness and a loss of interest by students in his teaching, caused him to resign his university post on a small pension in 1879.

The influence of Wagner

Nietzsche's dissatisfaction with the academic world is reflected in his work. Although he did write some scholarly articles in the 1860s, he was a reluctant adherent to the accepted norms of the academic style. Nietzsche always considered himself as something of a poet and a composer. He liked to improvise on the piano and wrote music himself. As a pupil at Pforta, Nietzsche formed a literary and musical society with some friends called 'Germania'. The friends would meet regularly to read aloud the works they had written or composed. Certainly, he saw his writing as an outlet for his artistic capabilities and indeed much (though not all) of his philosophy is extremely poetic and dramatic. Nonetheless, in his early work especially, this can come across as evidence of an immaturity and a deflection from any kind of rigorous scholarly coherency that would have been expected of a university professor. Coupled with this, his relationship and blind love for Wagner infected his early writing. Nietzsche does not really begin to find his own voice until his split from the composer.

Wagner was always a controversial and larger-than-life figure. Although he had already written four operas, it was *Tannhauser* in 1845 that caused the most controversy. Because of its innovations in structure and technique it both confused and shocked his audiences. He was also a political radical, taking an active part in the revolution in Germany in 1848, which required him to live in exile in Zurich where he started composing the famous *Ring* trilogy. The political ban against Wagner was lifted in 1861 and he returned to Prussia. Despite marrying an actress in 1836, Wagner had a number of affairs, most notably with the daughter of the composer Liszt, Cosima von Bulow. They married in 1870.

Wagner was more than a composer, however. He was also a musical theorist, and his thought on political issues such as nationalism and social idealism greatly influenced the nineteenth century. His music was strongly nationalist, and he had also expressed clear anti-Semitism in his writings, making him an attractive composer for the Nazis. Despite this reputation, Wagner did affect a revolution in the theory and practice of operatic composition and it was this factor that would have appealed to Nietzsche and his early belief that music acted as a salvation.

In retrospect it seems surprising that someone as perceptive as Nietzsche seemed to be so taken in by the flamboyant ego of Wagner. It is said that, during Nietzsche's weekend visits to Tribschen, Wagner would behave as if in one of his own operas. Dressed extravagantly, with only his own music playing, he would waft across the gardens and corridors of his luxurious villa amongst busts of himself, talking mostly about himself! However, this picture is most likely an exaggeration and Nietzsche did learn much from being in the company of Wagner, for he recognized the composer's ego as a need to dominate others, to exert his power over them. Undoubtedly, Wagner was a charismatic figure, and it is quite impressive what he could persuade others to do for him. From studying Wagner, Nietzsche developed his own views on psychology and on the desire for man to dominate others. In this respect, Wagner's eccentricities were a minor irritation. However, during the early Leipzig years, Nietzsche's infatuation with Wagner and his willingness to sacrifice his own career if need be to serve under the composer came across only too obviously in his early writings, especially with his first major work, *The Birth of Tragedy*. It was in Wagner's writings, especially in five essays published during 1849–51, that laid the basis for Nietzsche's early philosophy.

Wagner wrote a series of works discussing his views on the relationship between art and life. Some of the most significant in terms of influencing Nietzsche were:

- *Art and Revolution* (July 1849). Tracing the history of the arts, Wagner holds that the individual arts (music, drama, theatre etc.) were once a complete and perfect whole. This art form only existed in the tragic drama of ancient Athens and disappeared when they split into their various components. After that time, and up until the present day, people looked to philosophy rather than art for an understanding of their world. Art in its highest and most perfect form is, therefore, pre-Christian.

- *The Artwork of the Future* (September 1849). Here Wagner argues that all the greatest inventions of mankind, from language to society, are a product of the *volk* ('folk'). The *volk* is more than a collection of individuals; it is the submersion of individual identity and ego and the resulting expression of a mystical group consciousness. The highest expression of this *volk* consciousness is art, and Wagner makes a link between *volk* art and nature. Therefore, the future of artwork is for all artists of all types to put aside their own individuality and ego (rather ironic coming from Wagner!) and the result will be a true expression of nature as art!

- *Opera and Drama* (January 1851). A full-scale book. The composer sings the praises of his forthcoming opera *Nibelung's Ring* as an example of complete art and criticizes the opera of his contemporaries such as Rossini.

- *A Communication to my Friends* (August 1851). Wagner considers the faults and successes of his own previous works and explains why he feels the need for a new kind of musical drama. Wagner presents his own plan to produce a three-part musical drama – the *Ring* trilogy – as a model of perfect art. He advertises his intentions to present this work at some future festival.

The Bayreuth Festival of 1876

This festival became the Bayreuth Festival of 1876. The festival consisted of the complete first performance of Wagner's *Ring Cycle*. It is a significant event in that it marks Nietzsche's realization that Wagner was not the great saviour he had envisioned. Attending the festival, Nietzsche was later to remark that he found the whole performance indicative of Wagner's German nationalism and anti-Semitism: two things Nietzsche found particularly distasteful. However, in 1871 when *The Birth of Tragedy* was published, Nietzsche was still very firmly in the grip of Wagner's charisma.

Nietzsche saw *The Birth of Tragedy* (see Chapter 03) as a manifesto for change, as a call for a revolution. He believed that mankind had lost all sense of purpose and was clinging on to religious and philosophical views that were no longer credible. He called for a return to the principles of Greek tragedy and devoted the final third of the book to the praise of Wagner as the new tragedian. In this respect the book failed completely. It was attacked severely by academics although, not surprisingly, praised by Wagnerians. Nietzsche himself, in a preface to the book added in 1886, described it as badly written and confused. However, perhaps Nietzsche is too severe a critic of his own work. It has elements of originality and most importantly it raises the question of the importance of art in our understanding of the world and our place within it. Art, together with our instinctual side, can also provide us with insights that are not accessible through reason.

The more cynical critics of Nietzsche saw *The Birth of Tragedy* as little more than a publicity stunt for Wagner. Their criticisms are understandable in that there did seem to be some mutual back-patting going on. Wagner, for his part, introduced Nietzsche to his publisher, while Nietzsche devoted a good deal of his book towards promoting Wagner as the new revolutionary and laid the ground for the Bayreuth Festival. When, in 1872, Wagner left Tribschen and moved to Bayreuth, the relationship between the two mellowed. But Nietzsche, despite growing doubts, remained a Wagnerian. In fact, Nietzsche's publicizing for the composer did not stop there as is evident from the fourth of his *Untimely Meditations* written in 1876.

After a series of financial difficulties that were only resolved by the offer of a subsidy by King Ludwig, the festival was finally set for August 1876. The small town of Bayreuth was chosen, and Wagner engaged in an immense process of creative and exhausting industry to prepare for what was an incredible musical endeavour. In the summer of 1874, Nietzsche decided to visit Wagner's house. This was the worst time Nietzsche could have chosen, for Wagner was not ready for any interruptions as he had yet to complete his composition for the festival. Nietzsche annoyed Wagner intensely during this period, and it may well have been his intention, employing such seemingly deliberate tactics as carrying a score of Brahms with him (Wagner hated Brahms) and even playing it on Wagner's piano.

The festival was due to begin on 13 August and would consist of three complete cycles of *The Ring of Nibelung*. *The Ring* consists of a lengthy prelude, followed by three complete musical tragedies: a 14-hour saga in total. The inspiration for this new myth derives from a number of old sagas, mediaeval retellings and contemporary commentaries. Wagner's stated aim was to present his 'musical drama' (Wagner was clear that this was not an opera, which he considered to be an example of how decadent art had become) to the *volk*, an audience who would participate in the emotional purpose of the drama. He presented a vision of the Greek masses streaming in their thousands into the Athenian amphitheatre and he imagined the same for Bayreuth. As it turned out, however, the first performance consisted of just the kind of people who would attend an opera: emperors, kings, barons and the upper-middle classes. Not surprisingly, this audience hardly let their hair down to engage in ecstatic, mystical union.

Nietzsche, for his part, could have been at the centre of the whole enterprise if he had so wished, but he preferred to remain on the sidelines. He did sit through the first complete *Cycle*, but gave his tickets away for the rest of the festival; the second *Cycle* in late August and the third in early September. Nietzsche was later to write that his morose behaviour during the festival was because of his awareness that Wagner was not to be the saviour after all. However, although disillusionment with Wagner was most likely a factor, Nietzsche's increasing ill health at that time would not have suited the activities of a music festival.

The influence of Schopenhauer

Nietzsche's final meeting with Wagner was in Sorrento, Italy in 1876. Their meeting was brief and polite but it was obvious to both that the friendship was over. The year 1876 also marked Nietzsche's split from the influence of the German philosopher Arthur Schopenhauer (1788–1860). To understand Schopenhauer's and, indeed, Nietzsche's philosophy it helps to have a brief account of the main philosophical themes that acted as a backdrop to German philosophy of the time:

Philosophical background to Schopenhauer

The Greeks

Much of Ancient Greek philosophy, most notably the works of Plato, questioned the nature of existence: is what we can see with our senses (sight, touch, taste, hearing, feeling) actually what is? For example, you see trees and birds outside your window, but can you be sure that they really exist and they are what we see them to be? Plato held that the world that we perceive with our senses is only appearance. Things are not as they appear to be and we are often deceived into thinking we distinguish something when, in actual fact, we do not. In other words, our senses are unreliable. However, mankind has the gift of reason and it is with our rational capacity, our intellect, that we can determine what really exists.

This view that there are two worlds, the world or appearance and the world of reality, has also existed in many of the great religions and, inevitably, it has led to speculation over what the 'real' world consists of and how, if at all, it is possible to enter this real world.

It is a view that is known in philosophy as **dualism**. For Plato, we gain access to the real world through the exercise of reason; for many religions it is through faith or ritual practice. Plato was, therefore, a supporter of **rationalism**: he believed that the power of reason provides us with important knowledge about the world.

Descartes and Spinoza

The French philosopher Rene Descartes expressed this dualism in a simpler manner; there are only two existent things: **thinking substance** (soul) and **extended substance** (matter). Descartes, however, was not overly concerned with which is 'more real' than the other, and nor did he address the important issue of how two very different kinds of substance can possibly interact with each other. The Dutch philosopher Baruch Spinoza (1632–77) responded to Descartes' dualism with his **pantheism**. For Spinoza, soul and matter are not 'substances' for there is only one substance in the whole universe, and that is God. Soul and matter, therefore, are merely expressions of God.

Locke and Berkeley

The debate between Descartes and Spinoza took on another form with the British philosophers John Locke (1632–1704) and Bishop George Berkeley (1685–1753). Locke is regarded as the founder of the philosophical school known as **empiricism**: Our knowledge comes from our experience of the world; the mind at birth is a complete blank. In direct opposition to rationalism, Locke argued that all of our knowledge of the world comes through experience of the material world. There are just two sources of knowledge, **ideas of sensation** and **ideas of reflection**.

- **Ideas of sensation** are, at the basic level, when the mind, through the senses, perceives an object, colour and so on.
- **Ideas of reflection** are when the mind reflects upon the object that is perceived. This is when the subject thinks about the objects, exercises his imagination, and so on.

The point Locke is making here is that the 'ideas' of mind, whether ideas of sensation or ideas of reflection, have their basis in the material world, they are not innate. Berkeley wrote in opposition to sceptics such as Locke by raising the question that if, as Locke argues, our knowledge of the material world rests upon the ideas that we have in our heads, then why should we suppose that there is anything *but* the ideas in our heads? The material world would be unnecessary. If it did not exist then it would not change our ideas one bit. Berkeley, therefore, concludes that there is no such thing as matter, only mind. This conclusion makes Berkeley the founder of the philosophical school of modern **idealism**: the position that gives a key role to the mind in the constitution of the world as it is experienced.

The question arises, however, as to where the ideas in the mind come from, if not from matter? Berkeley states that the ideas from the mind come directly from God. For Berkeley, too, there are two kinds of ideas:

- Those that we have no control over, for example, sights and sounds that are forced upon our consciousness. As these are not a product of our will, then they must be a product of some other will, which is God.
- Those that we do have control over, for example, reflecting upon our ideas or exercising our imaginations.

Hume and Kant

The Scottish philosopher and empiricist David Hume (1711–76) asserted that our mind consists of **impressions** and **ideas**.

- **Impressions** are what Locke called 'ideas of sensation': objects, colours, sounds and so on, of the material world.
- **Ideas** are *images* of impressions that are formed from thinking and reasoning.

We can, therefore, have no ideas of anything unless we first receive an impression. For example, you may have an impression of fire and an impression of heat, you then form the idea in your mind that fire *causes* heat. However, Hume argues, the *causation* does not exist in reality, only in our minds. Causation is based upon past experience, but that does not mean that fire will cause heat in the future. At best, we can only *suppose* that it will.

When the German philosopher Immanuel Kant (1724–1804) read Hume, it changed his life and he set about developing the foundation of modern German philosophy that had a direct influence upon Schopenhauer and Nietzsche. Kant agreed with Hume that there are no innate ideas, but he did not accept that all knowledge is derived from experience. Whereas empiricism argues that our knowledge must conform to experience, Kant turned this around and argued that our experience must conform to our knowledge.

For example, an empiricist would argue that if you experience a stone falling to the floor many thousands of times then you suppose, based upon that experience, that it will fall to the floor the next time. It *may not*, of course, but it is the only knowledge we have to go on: our minds create the 'idea' that the stone will fall. Now, Kant is notoriously difficult and technical at the best of times, but put simply, he asks why we impose causation upon the stone. That is, why do we suppose that letting go of the stone will cause it to fall to the ground? Causation is not derived from the senses, and here Kant agrees with Hume, but then where *does* it come from? Kant argues that we humans impose an order upon the world; we impose causation, quantity, quality and so on, so that we may understand it. There are, therefore, two worlds:

- the world of **phenomena** or 'appearance'
- the world of **noumena** or 'reality'.

It is rather like wearing irremovable spectacles that make you see the world in a certain way. However, this is not how the world really is. The world of the noumenal we cannot see because we are limited in our perceptions. The inevitable conclusion Kant reached is that there is the world of appearance that we impose through our 'irremovable spectacles' and the world as it really is, which we cannot perceive.

Schopenhauer accepts Kant's view that there is a phenomenal world and a noumenal world. However, he believed that it *is* possible to know the noumenal:

- He equates the world of phenomena with Berkeley's ideas in the mind. Therefore, the world as it is perceived is the creation of the mind that perceives it. In other words, 'the world is my idea'.

- As Kant argues that if there is an 'apparent' world there must also be a real world, Schopenhauer equates the real world with the 'I' who has the idea.

Our knowledge of ourselves is obviously different from the knowledge we have of anyone or anything else. We know ourselves objectively in the same way we know other phenomena in the world; that is as a physical object, a body. We also have subjective knowledge, our inner consciousness, our feelings and desires. It is our inner selves that Schopenhauer calls 'Will'. Therefore, the body is part of the phenomenal world, the world of appearance, and the Will is in the noumenal form, the world of reality.

> Ideas   =   appearance   =   body and other objects
> The 'I' that has the idea   =   reality   =   Will

The world is a duality. *All* things have both will and idea, even a stone. However, in the case of the stone its Will has not attained a state of consciousness. Schopenhauer's concept of 'Will' should not be understood in the common sense as simply wanting something for oneself, but is much more than that. It is the essence of what it means to be human. Previous to Schopenhauer, much of the philosophical tradition places mankind as the thinking animal, as a rational, conscious being, but Schopenhauer saw consciousness as the mere surface of our minds. Under the conscious intellect is the unconscious will which is a striving, persistent force. On appearances it may seem that the intellect drives the will, but it is, in fact, the other way around. When you desire something it is not because you have found a good reason to desire it, but rather you desire something first and then establish reasons to cloak those desires. Therefore, it is pointless to appeal to people through logic. Rather, you must look to their desires, their self-interests.

Schopenhauer's pessimism

Every person embodies Will and the nature of Will is to survive. In the Darwinian sense of survival of the species, every individual is striving against the Will of others in a self-interested way. This inevitably results in conflict and suffering. Therefore, Schopenhauer sees the Will as essentially evil and the only way out of this suffering and evil is the denial of the Will, a refusal to take part in the egotistical contest for domination of others. This can be achieved through the power of the conscious intellect, which is able to comprehend the nature of the Will and its effects. The result, by denying the Will (which is the only reality) and being left with ideas (which are not real) is extinction of the self.

This philosophy now enters the realms of ascetic sainthood and Schopenhauer reveals the influence of Buddhism upon him. Nietzsche, like Wagner, initially accepted the view that we should 'deny the Will' although was later to doubt the practicality of such an activity. In fact, Schopenhauer himself was hardly the best model of the ascetic, for he loved the good life. Ultimately, the most important influence of Schopenhauer on Nietzsche amounts to three things:

- Like Schopenhauer, Nietzsche presented the picture of the philosopher who will stop at nothing in the search for truth, however painful that might be.
- Schopenhauer's style of writing, perhaps more than the content, had an influence on Nietzsche's own style and provided a demonstration that one can write philosophy and also write well.
- Nietzsche *seemingly* (see Chapter 05 for the debate on this) adopted the primacy of the will as the motivating force and this became the **will to power**.

However, Nietzsche's *will to power* is in many respects different from Schopenhauer's Will, and Nietzsche was much more materialistic (that is, 'down-to-earth') in his philosophy than Schopenhauer's almost mystical views. Both Wagner and Schopenhauer, therefore, played an important part in Nietzsche's early works, but this influence dwindles as Nietzsche develops his own voice.

Summary

- His father died when Nietzsche was only five years old and he lived in a house of female relatives.
- In early life, Wagner and Schopenhauer heavily influenced Nietzsche in the formation of his own philosophy.
- In August 1876 Nietzsche attends the first Bayreuth Festival. However, he leaves after the first performance. The same year, he breaks up with Wagner and rejects Schopenhauer's concept of the Will.
- Nietzsche was influenced by Schopenhauer's concept of the Will in the development of his own *will to power*.

02
Nietzsche's later life and death 1879–1900

In this chapter you will learn:

- about Nietzsche's friends
- about his retirement from teaching and his subsequent 'wanderings' and writing
- about his relationship with Lou Salome and Paul Rée
- about his final years
- about his sister, Elisabeth.

I am a wanderer and a mountain-climber (he said to his heart), I do not like the plains and it seems I cannot sit still for long. And whatever may yet come to me as fate and experience – a wandering and a mountain-climbing will be in it: in the final analysis one only experiences oneself.

(*TSZ*, Part Three, The Wanderer)

Malwida von Meysenbug (1816–1903) and Paul Rée (1849–1901)

When Nietzsche was at Bayreuth in 1872 he was introduced by Cosima Wagner to a good friend of the Wagners and a Schopenhauer advocate, Malwida von Meysenbug. Meysenbug was a fascinating character in her own right and her *Memoirs of an Idealist* are worth a read. She was a campaigner for democracy and womens' rights and had fought for political reform in Germany in 1848, resulting in a decade of exile in England. Wnen Meysenbug heard about Nietzsche's ill-health she recommended that he spend some time in Italy and so he took a year's leave of absence from Basel starting in the autumn of 1876. No doubt Nietzsche had been considering for some time resigning his post as professor of philology and becoming a 'free philosopher'; a stateless and wandering exile. As someone who knew his Latin and Greek from stuffy libraries, the desire to 'go south' must have been great. He didn't go alone, however, but was accompanied by the philosopher and friend Paul Rée and a 21-year-old Basel law student named Albert Brenner.

Meysenbug considered herself something of a mentor for young German writers and artists. Nietzsche, Rée and Brenner stayed in the Villa Rubinacci which had views over the sea to Naples and Vesuvius. Today, Villa Rubinacci is the name of the restaurant on Via Correale, although the actual villa Nietzsche stayed in is next door and is now known as the Hotel Eden. Back then the villa was located in a vineyard and catered for German visitors, and the three men had rooms on the first floor. At first, Nietzsche was uncomfortable, as Wagner had also decided to visit Italy and was staying at a hotel nearby. Nietzsche met up with Wagner a few times and such visits were cordial enough, but hardly inspiring. By this time, Wagner was a much older man (he was now 63) in Nietzsche's eyes and Nietzsche had outgrown him. Once Wagner left Italy, Nietzsche seemed to settle much better.

Nietzsche first met Rée in 1873 when the latter, as a non-student, chose to attend a series of lectures given by Nietzsche on The Pre-Platonic Philosophers. Rée was five years younger than Nietzsche and, by all accounts, much more precocious. Rée was the son of a Jewish landowner and was also an atheist, but his view of existence as having no ultimate meaning led Rée into pessimism, whereas it tended to liberate Nietzsche. Originally, Rée had been a law student but became attracted to philosophy, and also emphasized the importance of psychology as a way in to understanding the beliefs of human beings. More specifically, Rée was interested in the religious and moral beliefs of humans, explaining religious experience as an attempt to interpret the world, rather than as witness to an objective reality. Nietzsche was particularly influenced, however, by what Rée had to say about morality.

Nietzsche saw the villa as a 'monastery for free spirits' and later wrote, 'In Sorrento I shook off nine years of moss.' The three 'free sprits' worked on their books and they read (usually Rée would read aloud to Nietzsche) the works of the French moralists such as Montaigne, La Rochefoucauld and Vauvenargues. Inspired by Rée and the French, Nietzsche wrote aphorisms which were brought together and published as *Human, All Too Human* (1886) and *Daybreak* (1881). Rée, for his part, wrote *The Origin of the Moral Sensations*; a theme which has resonance in much of Nietzsche's own writing from this time on. The visit to Sorrento was undoubtedly a turning point for Nietzsche as it reinforced his decision to give up his professorial post and become a 'free spirit', but he was also set on finding himself a wife at this time and discussed this with Meysenbug. A letter he wrote to his sister Elisabeth on the topic while still in Sorrento is worth quoting:

We [Nietzsche and Meysenbug] are convinced that in the long run I shall have to give up my Basel university life, that if I continued there it would be at the cost of all my more important designs and would involve a complete breakdown of my health. Naturally I shall have to remain there during next winter, but I shall finish with it at Easter 1878, provided we bring off the other arrangement, i.e. marriage with a suitable and necessarily well-to-do-woman. 'Good *but* rich', as Frl. von M. [Meysenbug] says ... This project will be pushed ahead this summer, in Switzerland, so that I should come back to Basel already married. Various persons have been invited to come to Switzerland, among them several names that will be quite unfamiliar to you ...'

Nietzsche never actually carried out his 'project', but one thing he became more convinced of, and that was to end his academic career, especially as his health continued to deteriorate. In April of 1879 he suffered from severe, disabling headaches which exhausted him completely. Consequently he asked to be relieved of his teaching and, in June, he was retired on a small but manageable (given his meagre requirements) pension.

Nietzsche's 'wanderings'

Throughout much of his mature life, Nietzsche was godless, stateless, homeless and wifeless. For the next ten years (1879–89) Nietzsche, with only the clothes on his back and a trunk full of possessions, wandered through Italy, southern France and Switzerland. He had been advised by the doctor to seek more clement environments for his health, and this he attempted to do. Despite the illness, Nietzsche now started to produce his greatest, most mature works. These include *Dawn* (1880), which attacks the idea that morality has any objective basis, *The Gay Science* (1882), which first declares the death of God, and *Thus Spoke Zarathustra* (1885), which talks of the 'Superman'. Perhaps Nietzsche's finest work of all, *Beyond Good and Evil* (1886), brings together all of Nietzsche's philosophy in the most systematic way he ever gets, yet Nietzsche remained largely unknown and unread.

Nietzsche's 'wanderings' should not be seen as periods of isolation and solitude, of leading a hermit existence in the same way as Zarathustra's ten-year retreat to the mountains. Nietzsche continued to have close friends and even, it seems, a lover, during his ten-year spell. He could quite probably have ended a life of relative solitude if he had so wished, but the fact is he did not wish it and probably required periods of solitude as this suited his nature. There were times of melancholy and regret, of wishing for a loving wife and children, but this always seemed to pass as he embraced his philosophical enterprise with such passion.

Whilst he continued to have friends, undoubtedly these friends began to feel that Nietzsche was testing their friendship to the limits. As his friends got older, their responsibilities to family and other things took over and they had less time for the wandering idealist, however charismatic that figure may have been. An example of such a friend was Peter Gast. Gast's real name was Heinrich Köselitz, but he adopted the name of Gast when he began to work seriously as a composer. In 1875, Gast, seven years younger than Nietzsche, went to Basel to study and became something of Nietzsche's 'disciple'. He first became Nietzsche's secretary, writing down his work as Nietzsche dictated, but later it seems that Gast was actually in love with Nietzsche, if Gast's letters to a friend from 1879 to 1881 are anything to go by: 'I have never loved a man as I do *him*, not even my father ...'

For the sake of his health, Nietzsche went to Riva at Lake Garda in 1880. At that time Gast was nearby in Venice struggling to gain recognition as a composer but when Nietzsche told him he was at Riva, Gast packed his bags and joined him. Gast's letters tell us that this proved to be a trying and miserable time. The weather in Riva turned out to be bad, raining for much of the time, which prompted Gast to write to a friend:

Here it rains almost without ceasing. How Nietzsche –
who is sensitive to every cloud that appears in the sky –
is faring, you may imagine.

Nietzsche took advantage of Gast's love for him, which pushed
even his greatest disciple to his limits:

You have no idea what I endured ... how many a night I
lay down and tried to sleep and when I thought about
what had happened during the day, and saw that I had
done nothing for myself and everything for other people,
I was often seized with such rage that I threw myself into
contortions and called down death and damnation on
Nietzsche. I have hardly ever felt so bad as I did during
this time ... Then, when I had at last managed to go to
sleep at four or five in the morning, Nietzsche would
often come along at nine or ten and ask if I would play
Chopin for him.

Nietzsche spent the winter of 1880–81 in Genoa finishing his
work *Daybreak* and approached his old friend Carl van
Gersdorff with a proposal to travel together to Tunis. Gersdorff
first met Nietzsche in 1863 when the former – then a student
himself – had read an essay Nietzsche had written and was so
impressed he made a point of meeting him. Gersdorff, probably
under the influence of Nietzsche, became a 'Schopenhauerian' as
well as part of the Wagner entourage. Gersdorff and Nietzsche
would spend holidays together and Gersdorff also attended
some of Nietzsche's lectures along with Paul Rée. However,
when Nietzsche suggested that he and Gersdorff spend a couple
of years in Tunis together, Gersdorff was reluctant, and
Nietzsche himself changed his mind when war broke out there.
Nietzsche then considered travelling to Mexico, but this idea
never came to fruition.

During this time, Nietzsche was particularly excited over his
new work *Daybreak*, declaring that, 'This is the book with
which people are likely to associate my name.' And '... I have
produced one of the boldest and most sublime and most
thought-provoking books ever born out of the human brain and

heart.' But curiously, only two months after giving *Daybreak* such praise, he wrote to Rée describing the book as 'poor piecemeal philosophy'. What had taken place to make Nietzsche change his mind? An interesting experience occurred whilst Nietzsche was staying in Sils-Maria in the Upper Engadine mountains of Switzerland, which Nietzsche himself described:

> I shall now tell the story of Zarathustra. The basic conception of the work, the idea of eternal recurrence, the highest formula of affirmation that can possibly be attained – belong to the August of the year 1881: it was jotted down on a piece of paper with the inscription: '6,000 feet beyond man and time'. I was that day walking through the woods beside the lake of Silvaplana; I stopped beside a mighty pyramidal block of stone which reared itself up not far from Surlei. Then this idea came to me.

This 'idea' of the eternal recurrence (see Chapter 06) is described in a way that suggests an almost religious experience that Nietzsche had. In fact, in *Ecce Homo*, he elaborates more on this 'vision' which he calls an 'inspiration':

> If one had the slightest residue of superstition left in one, one would hardly be able to set aside the idea that one is merely incarnation, merely mouthpiece, merely medium of overwhelming forces. The concept of revelation, in the sense that something suddenly, with unspeakable certainty and subtlety, becomes visible, audible, simply describes the fact. One hears, one does not seek; one takes, one does not ask who gives; a thought flashes up like lightning, with necessity, unfalteringly formed – I have never had any choice. An ecstasy whose tremendous tension sometimes discharges itself in a flood of tears, while one's steps now involuntarily rush along, now involuntarily lag; a complete being outside oneself with the distinct consciousness of a multitude of subtle shudders and trickling down to one's toes ... Everything is in the highest degree involuntary but takes place as in

a tempest of a feeling of freedom, of absoluteness, of power, of divinity.

(*EH*)

This 'inspiration' is not conceived of in terms of ideas that Nietzsche himself invented, but rather it comes across as a mystical feeling 'of power, of divinity'. In the same book, when Nietzsche talks of his 'conception' of Zarathustra he says, 'It was on these two walks that the whole of the first Zarathustra came to me, above all Zarathustra himself, as a type: more accurately, *he stole up on me* …' Nietzsche described this experience in a letter to his friend Peter Gast, written in August 1881. He described his elation, and his tears: 'Not sentimental tears, mind you, but tears of joy, to the accompaniment of which I sang and talked nonsense, filled with a new vision far superior to that of other men.'

This experience is certainly significant, and any student of Nietzsche should be hesitant in describing him as lacking a spiritual side. Some have suggested that this experience is the first sign of Nietzsche's madness, but to suggest this is to discount all of his writings after *Daybreak* as the product of a madman when, in fact, he goes on to produce much more mature and philosophically rigorous work than previously. What the Surlej experience does tell us, however, is that Nietzsche saw himself as entering a new phase in his philosophical enterprise, a belief that he now had a 'calling' for want of a better term and would lead to *Thus Spoke Zarathustra*. In this sense we can say that Nietzsche looked to his earlier works as 'piecemeal philosophy'.

Lou von Salomé (1861–1937)

From 1882 Nietzsche's thoughts were already on *Zarathustra*, with Part One written by February 1883. Paul Rée had spent some time with Nietzsche in Genoa before heading off to Rome in March 1882. At the same time, Nietzsche curiously headed to Messina in Sicily. This is an unusual choice for Nietzsche as normally at that time of year he would head for more northerly climes. Whatever the reason, he seemed happy enough there, writing to Gast:

> So, I have arrived at 'my corner of the earth', where, according to Homer, happiness is said to dwell. Truly, I have never been in such good spirits as in the past week, and my fellow citizens are pampering and spoiling me in the most charming way.

Rée, for his part, stayed at the house of Meysenbug in Rome and there met the 20-year-old Lou Salomé; a woman Rée immediately fell in love with. Salomé was born in St Petersburg, the daughter of a Russian general of Huguenot descent. She left Russia in 1880 with her mother to study at the University of Zurich, but suffered from a severe lung disease that compelled her to look to better climates to recover. Her doctors, who only gave her a few years to live, suggested she head south and hence she ended up in the Meysenbug home. No doubt her feeling that she would not live long gave her an extra passion for life, and an enthusiasm for the study of philosophy that would have attracted many to her. It certainly had an effect on Rée as they would walk the streets of Rome night after night discussing their ideas. Rée was so excited about Salomé that he would write to Nietzsche about her. One response from Nietzsche is particularly interesting:

> Give that Russian girl my regards if that makes any sense: I lust after this kind of soul. Indeed I plan to go on the prowl for one quite soon; considering what I wish to accomplish in the next ten years, I need one. Marriage is an altogether different story – I could agree only to a maximum of two years of marriage.

Nietzsche seems to have had a purely pragmatic attitude towards marriage, more a case of needing someone to run the household and, more importantly, act as his amanuensis. Previously he had relied upon his friends for this and, apparently, had also acquired a typewriter which he complained bitterly about as being defective, although it is hard to imagine

Nietzsche – with his severe migraines – banging away at a typewriter. It would have made an interesting thesis to investigate whether Nietzsche's style altered as a result of using a typewriter, but alas no typewritten manuscripts of his seem to exist and so he probably never used one at all. Some words have also been written speculating about Nietzsche's sexuality, suggestions made that his pragmatic approach to marriage fits with homosexual tendencies. His unconventional visit to Messina has, in fact, been seen as an attempt to fulfil his homo-erotic fantasies, as Messina at the time was the home for a homosexual colony. Such speculation, however, must remain as nothing more than speculation unless further evidence comes to light.

Nietzsche certainly seemed to lack certain social skills when it came to marriage proposals. In April 1876 he proposed marriage to a woman he hardly knew, having met her only three times. He was promptly rejected, but this did not seem to overly bother Nietzsche. When Nietzsche, having spent three weeks in Messina, turned up in Rome in April 1882 it was only a matter of days before he proposed to Salomé. Rée had also proposed to Salomé but her response to both of them was that she was not interested in marriage, but would rather form a kind of intellectual *ménage à trois* in which the three of them would share an apartment in Vienna or Paris, writing, studying and debating. This idea certainly seemed to appeal to Nietzsche, who often dreamed of a 'secular monastery'.

Such a threesome was bound to fail eventually, given the egos and competitive nature of the three characters. But the *ménage à trois* did not occur immediately, rather Salomé spent some time with Rée and his mother in West Prussia before, in August, spending three weeks in Tautenburg with Nietzsche and his sister Elisabeth. Nietzsche's sister took a dislike to Salomé and considered the idea of such a threesome insane. At Tautenburg, Salomé and Nietzsche were housed in separate apartments and they would take long walks together. Whilst she loved the conversations, she did not love Nietzsche, and wrote:

In some deep dark corner of our beings we are worlds apart. Nietzsche's nature is like an old castle that conceals within it many a dark dungeon and hidden basement room, not apparent at first glance and yet likely to contain all the essentials. It is strange, but recently the idea suddenly struck me that we could wind up facing each other as enemies someday.

Salomé's prediction was later to prove correct, as evidenced from a letter Nietzsche wrote (but never sent) to Paul Rée's brother, in July 1883: 'This scrawny dirty smelly monkey with her fake breasts – a disaster!'

In the meantime, however, plans were drawn to set up the *ménage à trois* in Paris. Nietzsche made inquiries amongst his friends in Paris regarding accommodation, but what he had not realized was that Rée had become increasingly jealous of Nietzsche in the relationship. Realizing that Nietzsche presented a possible threat to his own romantic intentions towards Salomé, Rée arranged for himself and Salomé to live far away from Nietzsche in Berlin. Nietzsche was never to see either of them again.

The final years

Undoubtedly the realization that he had been ditched, that he had been taken in by a 21-year-old, had an emotional effect upon Nietzsche. For solace, Nietzsche now buried himself in his work *Thus Spoke Zarathustra*. Reading the opening pages of *Zarathustra* we can see this as autobiographical, as it paints a picture of the suffering and solitude that Nietzsche himself now felt. Nietzsche felt alone in the world. For company he turned to his sister who made every effort to ruin the name of Salomé by writing letters decrying her character and her 'immoral' lifestyle with Rée. Nietzsche, it seemed, may well have been party to this dung-throwing.

The year 1888 was the last of Nietzsche's sane life and, ironically, the first of his fame. He spent the beginning of that fateful year in Nice, stayed in Turin from April till June, spent the summer in Sils-Maria, and then returned to Turin in September. It was, in this respect, a year of his usual wanderings. But, in other respects, it was very different. In his correspondence, Nietzsche reported that his health was improving and he felt a sense of joy and elation with life, not recognizing that these feelings of euphoria were symptomatic of forthcoming megalomania.

Added to this tragedy was the fact that Nietzsche was never to appreciate the success and influence his work was to have, for undoubtedly Nietzsche courted notoriety and wanted success. It was on the very first day of 1888 that the first ever review of Nietzsche's whole work appeared in a German newspaper. A few months later, in April, the internationally renowned Danish critic and biographer Georg Brandes (1842–1927) gave a series of successful lectures on Nietzsche at Copenhagen University. Nietzsche had finally arrived, yet his letters were becoming more and more bizarre, evidence of the oncoming insanity.

In this final year, Nietzsche was as prolific a writer as ever. He wrote six short books: *The Wagner Case*; *The Twighlight of the Idols*; *The Antichrist*; *Ecce Homo*; *Nietzsche contra Wagner* and *Dithyrambs of Dionysus*. So are these works in any way a reflection of Nietzsche's coming insanity? In these works he does not introduce any new philosophy and nor does he contradict what he has previously said. There is evident continuation from his previous work and the structure is generally tight and presented in a magnificent poetic style. These works deserve attention, therefore, and show no evidence of Nietzsche having lost his intellectual capacity. Quite the contrary, in fact.

On 3 January 1889, according to a well-known although possibly apocryphal account, Nietzsche walked out of his lodgings and saw in the piazza a cabman beating his horse. Nietzsche cried out, ran across the square and threw his arms around the neck of the horse. At that moment he lost consciousness. A crowd gathered and the landlord of Nietzsche's lodgings carried the still unconscious Nietzsche back to his room. When he finally came to, he shouted, sang and punched away at the piano. When he calmed down he wrote a series of epistles to his friends and the courts of Europe declaring that he, 'the crucified', would be going to Rome in five days' time and that all the princes of Europe and the Pope should assemble.

Nietzsche was now permanently insane. One of his few remaining friends, Overbeck, disturbed by the letters, went to Turin and persuaded Nietzsche to come to Basel. He was taken to a clinic in Jena, near the home of his mother. At the clinic, Nietzsche behaved like an imperious ruler, surveying the premises as if it were his palace. His conversation would switch from the rational to the nonsensical and violent at any given moment. When it was clear that no improvement was possible, Nietzsche was allowed to be housed with his mother at Naumburg. She looked after him devotedly until her death in 1897. For seven years she watched him night and day fall into a steady decline and apathy. It was unfortunate that the care of Nietzsche until his own death on 25 August 1900 was to be in the hands of his sister Elisabeth.

Elisabeth Förster-Nietzsche (1846–1935)

Much of Nietzsche's legacy is closely related to his sister's less favourable legacy. Elisabeth Nietzsche, more than any other person, is responsible for the misunderstandings that have accompanied Nietzsche's philosophy to this day. When Nietzsche started writing poetry at the age of eight, it was the six-year-old Elisabeth who collated them for him. At such an early age she already felt responsible for the work and life of the shy Friedrich.

Elisabeth loved the first Bayreuth Festival in 1876; the event that Nietzsche hated so much. She had already got to know Wagner through her brother and she was captivated by his anti-Semitic ideas. At the festival she met and fell in love with Bernhard Förster, an anti-Semitic fanatic who was also addicted to Wagner's writings on Jews. Förster saw in Wagner a guide that would help him to become a professional anti-Semite, a member of the notorious 'German Seven' who called for the registration of Jews and the stop on Jewish immigration. Much to the disgust of Nietzsche, Förster married Elisabeth who, for her part, attempted unsuccessfully to recruit her brother into the anti-Semitic cause.

Wagner once wrote of the possibility of establishing a pure German colony in South America where Jews would be banned. This idea, even though Wagner himself knew little about South America, was taken up by Bernhard Förster with great enthusiasm. He formed a group of somewhat disparate disciples and they, together with Elisabeth, sailed off to Paraguay where they established a colony called New Germany in 1887. New Germany exists to this day; consisting of around 200 Germans (sharing 11 surnames) it continues to uphold the language, culture and practices of nineteenth-century German peasantry.

As for Bernhard Förster, he grew increasingly in debt and committed suicide the same year that Nietzsche went mad. Nietzsche's madness was the excuse Elisabeth needed to abandon New Germany to its fate, and pursue her new full-time mission of making her brother famous. For the next 40 years, Elisabeth manipulated his works and superimposed her own racist views upon it.

The Nietzsche Archive

On returning to Germany, Elisabeth – who represented everything that Nietzsche hated about Germany and Germans – became his 'guardian' and owner of his copyrights. Immediately, Elisabeth set about taking control of all of Nietzsche's writings. When Nietzsche collapsed in madness he left behind mounds of unpublished material at his various lodgings. Elisabeth established an 'archive' in a house in Naumburg that would become a museum of Nietzsche's works. As well as his works, however, Nietzsche himself was lodged in a room as one of the exhibits. Incapable of coherent speech, he was exhibited to important visitors and dressed in a white robe like a Brahman priest. Elisabeth turned her brother into a prophet, surrounding him in mystique and turning his madness into something superhuman.

In 1896 Elisabeth moved the growing Archive to Weimar, considered the cultural centre of Germany. In fact, during World War II, Weimar was the centre for cultural propaganda, with Nietzsche as the official philosopher of Nazism. When the Russians occupied Weimar after the war, the Archive was sealed and remained so until the fall of the Berlin Wall in 1989.

The collected works of Nietzsche brought Elisabeth fame and fortune and she became the official mouthpiece for her brother. However, in collecting his works, she would ignore any of his philosophy that she did not agree with, forge letters that she claimed Nietzsche had written to her that praised her, and wrote a popular biography of Nietzsche that was full of lies. The greatest sin of all was that she collected Nietzsche's unpublished notes into a book called the *will to power*. She claimed that this was Nietzsche's final testament, his true philosophy, whereas it is full of discarded thoughts and poorly written notes that Nietzsche had no intention of publishing. Although of historical interest, it is a shame that it is still quoted as an authority of Nietzsche's philosophy.

Nietzsche, at a time before his mental collapse and the fall-out with his sister, had once written to Elisabeth requesting that, at his death – for he always believed he would die young – he should be given a pagan burial, with no priest at his grave. However, when he died on 25 August 1900, Elisabeth gave him a full Lutheran funeral and buried him in a coffin with a silver cross.

Summary

- Due to his illness, Nietzsche was compelled to give up his lecturing post and spent the rest of his life travelling and writing.
- He continued to have a number of friends and possibly a lover in Lou Salomé.
- However, he became increasingly isolated.
- He went mad in 1889 and died in 1900.

03

The Birth of Tragedy

In this chapter you will learn:

- about the reception of Nietzsche's first major work *The Birth of Tragedy*
- about his teachings on Apollo and Dionysus
- about his criticisms of the 'theoretical man'.

My time has not yet come, some are born posthumously. One day or other institutions will be needed in which people live and teach as I understand living and teaching: perhaps even chairs for the interpretation of Zarathustra will be established.

(*EH*, Why I Write Such Excellent Books)

Nietzsche certainly was 'born posthumously' in the sense that his first major work, *The Birth of Tragedy*, fell upon deaf ears when it was published and yet is now considered to be an inspired account of Greek tragedy and is studied in many universities across the world. Despite Nietzsche's acknowledged brilliance and precociousness, this first work did not help to cement that reputation in academic circles; in fact it did more harm than good. Its publication was heavily criticized by scholars. For example, the young scholar Ulrich von Wilamowitz-Möllendorf (1848–1931) attacked Nietzsche's book in a 32-page pamphlet with the sarcastic title *Philology of the Future*. Sarcastic maybe, but the point was made that Nietzsche was being far too ambitious, visionary, and lacking the limited – some would say 'dry' – pragmatism of academia.

Nietzsche's dissatisfaction with the academic world is reflected in his work as he either refused or was unable to write within the accepted norms of the academic style. Nietzsche always considered himself as something of a poet and a composer. As a pupil at Pforta, Nietzsche formed a literary and musical society with some friends called 'Germania'. The friends would meet regularly to read aloud the works they had written or composed. Certainly, he saw his writing as an outlet for his artistic capabilities and, indeed, much (though not all) of his philosophy is extremely poetic and dramatic. Nonetheless, in his early work especially, this can come across as evidence of an immaturity and a deflection from any kind of rigorous scholarly coherency that would have been expected of a university professor. Coupled with this, his relationship and blind love for Wagner infected his early writing, and Nietzsche does not really begin to find his own voice until his split from the composer. Needless to say Wagner considered *The Birth of Tragedy* a wonderful piece of work, but this is hardly surprising considering how much praise it heaps upon the composer.

The 'theoretical man'

The Birth of Tragedy deserves a chapter of its own because the work itself stands out as a unique and interesting thesis. A first impression may make one wonder why Nietzsche chose to consider Greek tragedy given his intention to produce a work that would have contemporary cultural significance, but this ignores the importance of Greek culture at the time of Nietzsche. It was not, then, as it may be seen by many today (quite wrongly), a 'dead' subject with little importance except for those who had the luxury to study it. Whilst on the one hand there was a push towards industrialization and market-place values, there was, on the other hand, an increase in disillusionment with the goals and values of modernity accompanied by a looking-back to bygone eras, most notably that of Ancient Greece. It was felt by many, poets and artists chief amongst them, that the Greeks possessed a set of values, a spirituality, and an affirmation of life that seemed to be desperately lacking amongst industrialized, scientific, modern man. This condemnation of modernity was something Nietzsche shared in, and the following passage from *The Birth of Tragedy* is particularly enlightening:

> Our whole modern world is caught in the net of Alexandrian culture, and the highest ideal it knows is *theoretical man*, equipped with the highest powers of understanding and working in the service of science, whose archetype and progenitor is Socrates. The original aim of all our means of education is to achieve this ideal; every other form of existence has to fight its way up alongside it, as something permitted but not intended.
>
> (*BT*, 18)

The 'theoretical man', the man of science and progress, is what Nietzsche consistently condemns until the end of his writing career, and it certainly possesses modern-day concerns where success is measured by how much money and property you possess rather than by, for want of a better word, 'wisdom'.

Interestingly, Nietzsche presents Socrates as an example of this 'theoretical man'. In the philosophical realm, Socrates is considered one of the greatest philosophers, yet Nietzsche frequently criticizes him as the 'archetype' of those modern, alienating values. Little is known about the life of Socrates and, as he did not write anything down, we have to rely on the writings of his disciple Plato who used Socrates as his mouthpiece in his dialogues. Therefore, when Nietzsche talks of the philosophy of Socrates he is not making any distinction with that of the philosophy of Plato. There were certain aspects of the philosophy of Socrates and Plato that Nietzsche particularly was in disagreement with.

Firstly, the Platonic view that there is such a thing as objective truth. This was a response to the belief in **relativism**: that the morals and beliefs are a product of a particular time and place and, therefore, there is no such thing as 'right' and 'wrong'. Secondly, Plato argued that the world we live in is essentially an illusion, a poor image of a better, perfect world. The role of the philosopher, therefore, was to seek out this world rather than be pre-occupied with everyday existence. Thirdly, Plato believed that the true world can be accessed through the power of *reason*. Mankind is both instinctual and rational and can choose to be instinctual and irrational like other animals, but mankind also has the gift of reason. By exercising reason – the intellect – mankind can know what truth is. Finally, Nietzsche lays the blame of over 2000 years of this kind of philosophy and the death of tragedy at the foot of Socrates. In particular the whole philosophical concern with **metaphysics**, the speculation on what exists beyond the physical world, Nietzsche considered to be an error and a distraction from what really mattered.

For Socrates, tragedy was no longer required because reason could remove the fear of death. Although Nietzsche admired the genius of Socrates, as well as his achievements, he saw Socrates as representative of the desire to *explain*, to engage in argument and counter-argument, rather than accept that ultimately there are no explanations. Also, Nietzsche was not against reason and science; he would be the first to praise its achievements and its role in the enhancement of life. What he condemned was the regard of reason as providing *answers*, as delivering mankind from a state of ignorance.

Despite Nietzsche's solitude and bouts of depression, he always argued for an affirmation of life, of saying 'yes' to life, rather than adopting the resigned cynicism of, say, Schopenhauer. This quality, he believed, existed amongst the Ancient Greeks, although they had much to complain about given the severity of existence for most of them, certainly in comparison to the luxury of modern European man. Nietzsche talked often of the importance of 'health', especially in conjunction with southern climes. These themes can be traced right back to *The Birth of Tragedy*.

When Nietzsche was only 23 he had written to a friend that he hoped one day to combine philology with music, to produce music that is written with words rather than with notes. To do this he needed a theme, and that of Greek tragedy seemed to fit the bill perfectly. Before starting to write *The Birth of Tragedy* he had already set his stage, having given two public lectures in 1870. The first of these lectures, 'Greek Music Drama', which examined Dionysian festivals as the origin of tragedy, was well-received and kept well within the framework of classical philology of the time, but Nietzsche wanted to be much more ambitious than that! The second lecture, 'Socrates and Tragedy', according to Nietzsche, 'aroused terror and misconceptions'. How, one wonders, could a public lecture 'arouse terror'? This lecture, in line with what he was intent on saying in *The Birth of Tragedy*, was Nietzsche's first public condemnation of the great Socrates. It focuses on the Greek philosopher's emphasis on rationalism as leading to the death of tragedy and, in Nietzsche's eyes, of wisdom. This dialectical will to knowledge destroyed the life forces of myth, religion and art. In this lecture, Nietzsche also suggests the possibility of a rebirth of Greek tragedy, although he does not at this point mention Wagner as this possible saviour.

It should be mentioned briefly that in talking of suffering, Nietzsche was by no means ignorant of how cruel and brutal the world can be. When Nietzsche wrote his essay *The Dionysian Worldview* in 1870, the Franco-Prussian War had just been declared. Rather than remain in his cloistered ivory tower, Nietzsche voluntarily enlisted as a medical orderly (an action that Cosima Wagner advised against, suggesting he send the soldiers cigars rather than himself). Nietzsche, at the very least, did experience war at first hand, limited though it was. As a medical orderly he witnessed scenes of appalling suffering and destruction. In a letter to Wagner he provides a graphic account of travelling for three days and nights in a cattle truck with the wounded. As it turned out, however, he only spent two weeks in September of 1870 on the battlefields before contracting dysentery and diphtheria.

Apollo and Dionysus

It has already been mentioned (see Chapter 01) that Wagner's writings had a huge influence on Nietzsche's early work. Wagner held that there is a dualism between, on the one hand, mankind and Nature and, on the other hand, Art and Nature. In *The Artwork of the Future* he argued that mankind, by exercising his intellect, is actually being drawn away from Nature and, therefore, his true Art. The fulfilled person is one who is in touch with his true nature and can express this through the medium of the perfect Art. Here Wagner is making parallels between the role and function of Art with religion. It is perhaps inevitable that when Wagner talks of his own art as being the model for the perfect, then – as the composer for this art – Wagner must be a religious 'saviour'.

In *The Birth of Tragedy*, Nietzsche gave a lot of importance to Art as a medium through which we comprehend the world. He took on board this dualism of Art and Nature under the principles of Apollo and Dionysus. These two Greek gods are presented as a metaphor for two fundamental principles:

- **The Apollonian:** Nietzsche compares the Apollonian with dreams. In a dream you express fantasies but these are a way of forgetting the world rather than confronting the realities of the world. Apollonian art is exemplified by painting and sculpture. In the same way that we conjure up images in dreams, we do the same in painting. But these paintings are only representations of the world; they are fantasies that allow us to turn our backs, at least for a while, from the world we live in. Apollo, then, is an artistic style: that of form and clarity, and so is also represented in sculpture and architecture most commonly.

- **The Dionysian:** Nietzsche compares Dionysian art with intoxication. Nietzsche did not necessarily mean alcoholic intoxication, but rather the kind of ecstasy that can also be caused by means other than alcohol, for example, through sexual intercourse, dancing or religious activities. Like the Apollonian, the Dionysian is a mechanism for fleeing from reality, but intoxication is not the same as fantasy. Dream fantasies are an individual and private experience when you turn away from the world. Dionysian intoxication, however, is not about forgetting the world, but forgetting your *self* and experiencing more of a mystical communal union. Dionysian art is more akin to music and poetry. Nietzsche accepted that the distinction between painting and music was not always so clear. It is quite possible, for example, to have Dionysian painting, and Nietzsche was aware that music had Apollo as its patron god. The more important distinction is how one *responds* to the work of art, rather than the work of art itself. Nietzsche sees Apollo as expressing individuality, whereas the Dionysian revels in music and dance and so breaks down the individual like some kind of Sufi *dhikr*.

A way of understanding what these Dionysian energies are like can be ascertained from the following:

From all corners of the ancient world (leaving aside the modern one in this instance), from Rome to Babylon, we can demonstrate the existence of Dionysiac festivals of a type which, at best, stands in the same relation to the Greek festivals as the bearded satyr, whose name and attributes were borrowed from the goat, stands to Dionysus himself. Almost everywhere an excess of sexual indiscipline, which flooded in waves over all family life and its venerable statutes, lay at the heart of such festivals. Here the very wildest of nature's beasts were unleashed, up to and including that repulsive mixture of sensuality and cruelty which has always struck me as the true 'witches' brew'. Although news of these festivals reached them by every sea- and land-route, the Greeks appear, for a time, to have been completely protected and insulated from their feverish stirrings by the figure of Apollo, who reared up in all his pride, there being no more dangerous power for him to confront with the Medusa's head than this crude, grotesque manifestation of the Dionysiac. Apollo's attitude of majestic rejection is eternalized in Doric art.

(*BT*, 2)

The Dionysiac energies, therefore, when unleashed are dangerous, grotesque, cruel, sexual and wild. It is the rule of the jungle: eat or be eaten. In such a vision of a conflicting, violent world it is difficult to find meaning or value or beauty but, for Nietzsche, this did not mean a path towards nihilism. Rather, his 'affirmation' – like the Greeks – is to revel in this energy. In a Schopenhauerian sense, the Dionysian represents the primary, cruel, creative and elemental life force that Schopenhauer refers to as 'will'. This gives Nietzsche's work an almost metaphysical dimension as he pictures the world of consisting of an underlying life force that is 'cultured' by societies that attempt to live within this violent, anarchic and uncaring force. Culture, then, is when human beings build up a liveable framework in which to survive in what is, in essence, a hostile climate, and some cultures, notably the Ancient Greeks, so far as Nietzsche was concerned, do this better than others.

The importance of culture

The importance of culture is another theme that remains throughout all of Nietzsche's works. When Nietzsche was at Basel in 1869 he met, and became acquainted with ('friend' would be too strong a word in this case as Burckhardt for his part kept his distance), the historian Jakob Burckhardt, whose most famous work, *The Culture of the Renaissance in Italy*, was published in 1860. Burckhardt, also something of a pessimistic Schopenhauerian, was particularly interested in the history of culture, as opposed to military or political history, and he argued for three major forces of existence: state, religion and culture. For Nietzsche, culture (which in his case could well include religion) was the highest objective, more so than, say, economics or science.

Nietzsche stresses that Apollo and Dionysus are not opposites, but work side by side. They complement each other and, therefore, the perfect Art (in the Wagnerian sense) is one that embodies both the Apollonian and the Dionysian. Like Wagner, Nietzsche saw this Art as existing in Greek tragedy. Nietzsche's most important contribution in *The Birth of Tragedy* is the attack on the view – prevalent among the middle classes of the time – that Ancient Greece was so idyllic. Rather, Nietzsche argued, the Greek way of life was brutal, short and full of suffering. How did the Greeks cope with these facts of life? Greek art, through the fusion of the Apollonian and the Dionysian, was such a mechanism for making life tolerable.

The Apollonian element was needed to create the illusion, the fantasy, which distracted them from the horrors of everyday life. If, Nietzsche argued, the Greeks were supposed to be as happy and sunny as pictured, then there would be no need for Apollonian art, yet there is plenty of evidence of Greek tragedy to show that the Greeks suffered immensely. In Greek tragedy we are presented with the images of gods and men, of heroes and monsters, as a way of transforming their fears for such things, in the same way dreams are projections of our own fears and doubts. The Dionysian element is the tragic chorus present in the tragedy. The chorus would narrate the story through song. The chorus acted as an artistic substitute for the Dionysian rites by allowing the audience to identify themselves with these singing, dancing characters and therefore participate within the tragedy themselves and not be mere spectators. This was therapeutic, allowing audiences to feel a sense of unity with their fellows, with the chorus, and with the drama of the tragedy as well as to feel god-like themselves.

Nietzsche's participation in the Franco-Prussian War, brief though it was, tells us something about Nietzsche and his views on war at this early age. When reading Nietzsche it is notable that he often uses militaristic terms and this has served to hinder an understanding of his philosophy while encouraging those who wish to interpret Nietzsche as a philosopher of war and military conquest. Nietzsche had initially hailed the Franco-Prussian War, seeing it as a catalyst for the revival of culture. As he wrote to one of his friends after deciding to take part in the war: '... we will once again need monasteries.' But Nietzsche was not being nationalistic in any way for he later distanced himself from the war when he realized that its primary motive was often more in line with profit-making and state-making. Rather he saw war as part of the inevitable ingredient of culture-making.

An interesting essay that was originally intended to be part of *The Birth of Tragedy* is 'The Greek State' which he printed privately and sent a copy to Cosima Wagner. More will be said of this essay when looking at Nietzsche's politics (see Chapter 09), but for now it is worth noting that in this short work he argues that the state emerges from attempts to subdue war within its own frontiers and rather directs it outwards. The formation and continued existence of states requires that there will always be wars between these states, but in the 'intervals' society has breathing space to produce 'the radiant blossoms of genius' of culture in 'the concentrated effect of that *bellum* [warfare], turned inward' ('The Greek State', 7, 344). Nietzsche was influenced by Burkhardt who had argued that culture arises from agony, and Nietzsche developed this line of thinking in arguing that war was a necessity for culture to thrive in what he calls the association of 'battlefield and artwork' ('The Greek State', 7, 344).

Life is tragic and in *The Birth of Tragedy* Nietzsche wrote a phrase that has often been quoted since: 'Existence and the world are eternally justified solely as an aesthetic phenomenon' (*BT*, 5). A *moral* point of view may well argue for democracy and the welfare state, for the greatest happiness for the greatest number, but an *aesthetic* point of view – which Nietzsche advocates – is not concerned with such 'levelling'. If we are looking for recurrent themes in Nietzsche, then undoubtedly a key theme is his criticism of modernity, of the way we are now. This criticism rests upon two key features of modernity. First, we have lost what he calls our 'metaphysical solace' when faced with the certainty of death. Second, we have killed myth. In this sense Nietzsche does not comes across at all as a post-modern existentialist, but more of a traditionalist calling out for traditional, indeed, *ancient* values. Nietzsche says that the modern man is a myth-less man; when, for example, we go to the theatre we can no longer experience the 'miracle' which, for children, is a matter of course (*BT* 23). We have lost the magic – in particular of art – because we have become critical-historical; the deconstructive spirit.

In the first essay of *Untimely Meditations* (1873), for example, Nietzsche is critical of the Hegelian David Strauss. This is because Strauss wrote a 'deconstructive' *Life of Jesus* in 1835–6. History, as Nietzsche points out in his second *Untimely Meditation*, is not to be understood as '*events* in the past', but rather '*representations* of the past'. Whilst history of the right sort is essential for life, history of the wrong sort kills life. By 'life', Nietzsche means the growth of a people, a community, a culture. The mistake Strauss made was to write the wrong kind of history, to deconstruct a monumental figure. Strauss, by attempting to present an objective, scientific history, kills history and kills religion by presenting it as false, crude, irrational and absurd. Life, for Nietzsche, is only possible if we have illusion; religion is only alive if we have illusion. There is a place for science – at times Nietzsche was very positive about scientific progress – and there is a place for religion, but there is no place for a science of religion. There's a wonderful remark from Bernard Nightingale in Tom Stoppard's *Arcadia*. He says:

> Why does scientific progress matter more than personalities? ... don't confuse progress with perfectibility. A great poet is always timely. A great philosopher is an urgent need. There's no rush for Isaac Newton. We were quite happy with Aristotle's cosmos. Personally, I preferred it. Fifty-five crystal spheres geared to God's crankshaft is my idea of a satisfying universe. I can't think of anything more trivial than the speed of light ...'

Nietzsche, for sure, would have seconded this.

The value of Greek tragedy

Nietzsche portrayed Greek tragedy as an interactive, mystical and unifying experience that provided a therapeutic outlet for a people who were sensitive to the suffering and uncertainties of everyday life and in which mankind is in tune with Nature. Man is no longer an artist but a work of art. Art possesses form and so by making life a work of art it gives the world a form, a structure. Nietzsche quotes the greatest tragedians as being Sophocles and Aeschylus in the fifth century BC. However, the other tragedian who is often associated with these two, Euripides, Nietzsche sees as the enemy of great Art.

Nietzsche argued that Euripides rid Greek drama of the role of the chorus, of the Dionysian element. The chorus became less central to the drama and became a matter of mere convention. Euripides, Nietzsche believed, killed tragedy. Nietzsche characterizes Euripides as a rational man and could not see what the seemingly irrational function of the chorus had. When Wagner wrote of mankind turning away from Art and towards philosophy, Nietzsche saw this as a movement away from the instinctual natural element towards the distant rational capacity. There is now an opposition between Dionysus and Socrates. Socrates, like Euripides, emphasizes the importance of reason and in the belief that, through the power of reason, we can gain access to truth. Nietzsche always placed a greater emphasis on the irrational and the instinctual and also believed that there is no such thing as 'truth'. Great art is no 'truer' than science or religion but Nietzsche believed art could at least put mankind in touch with Nature and his fellow Man. It is an acceptance that there is only this life and it is full of suffering, rather than a belief that there is a better, pain-free life.

What has this got to do with the modern European that Nietzsche was addressing? Although the Ancient Greeks suffered, Classical Greek tragedy, Nietzsche believed, presents a balanced picture of the world. Whilst understanding that individuals inevitably suffer in this life, there is solace in being aware of the underlying energies that pervade the world. As mentioned, Nietzsche saw Socrates as the precursor of an alternate, disabling, vision of 'optimism': an over-rationalized, logical, scientific view of the world that represses the emotions, the human instincts. At this time, and remember Nietzsche was only 28, he saw *The Birth of Tragedy* as a manifesto for change, as a call for a revolution. While such rhetoric is rarely the place for an academic text, it was heartfelt, hence Nietzsche's frustrations with dusty academia. He was also still in the grips of Schopenhauer and Kant to a large extent, and saw their philosophical enterprises as a break away from Socratic 'optimism'. The resurrection of the Greek worldview was also present, Nietzsche thought, in music:

> From the Dionysiac ground of the German spirit a power has risen up which has nothing in common with the original conditions of Socratic culture and which can neither be explained not excused by these conditions; rather, this culture feels it to be something terrifying and inexplicable, something overpowering and hostile, namely German music, as we see it in the mighty, brilliant course it has run from Bach to Beethoven, from Beethoven to Wagner. What can the knowledge-lusting

Socratism of today hope to do with this daemon as it emerges from unfathomable depths?

(*BT*, 19)

At this point in Nietzsche's philosophical career he was not only under the influence of Wagner, but he was also still Schopenhauerian and Kantian in his outlook. To their credit, which Nietzsche acknowledges, both these philosophers shared in Nietzsche's own enterprise in putting limits to the perceived unbounded scope of the scientific enterprise. Reason alone could not, after all, provide all the answers. He believed that mankind had lost all sense of purpose and was clinging on to religious and philosophical views that were no longer credible. He called for a return to the principles of Greek tragedy and devotes the final third of the book to the praise of Wagner as the new tragedian. In this respect the book failed completely.

The Birth of Tragedy was attacked severely by academics although, not surprisingly, praised by Wagnerians. Nietzsche himself, in a preface to the book added in 1886, described it as badly written and confused:

> I repeat: I find it an impossible book today. I declare that it is badly written, clumsy, embarrassing, with a rage for imagery and confused in its imagery, emotional, here and there sugary to the point of effeminacy, uneven in pace, lacking the will to logical cleanliness, very convinced and therefore too arrogant to prove its assertions, mistrustful even in the propriety of proving things [... and so on ...].
>
> (*BT*, An Attempt at Self-Criticism)

However, perhaps Nietzsche is too severe a critic of his own work. It has elements of originality and most importantly it raises the question of the importance of Art in our understanding of the world and our place within it. Art, together with our instinctual side, can also provide us with insights that are not accessible through reason.

Summary

• Nietzsche's first major work was *The Birth of Tragedy*. It was greatly influenced by the writings of Wagner on the importance of Art.

• *The Birth of Tragedy* argues the following:

The perfect Art is a combination of fantasy (Apollo) and intoxication (Dionysus).

This perfect Art existed in Ancient Greek tragedy.

That Euripides and Socrates are to blame for the death of the perfect Art.

A return to the age of perfect Art needs to be achieved and Wagner is cited as an example.

• *The Birth of Tragedy* was severely criticized by scholars.

04

the revaluation of all values

In this chapter you will learn:

- what is meant by 'morality'
- what Nietzsche means when he says, 'God is dead'
- about Nietzsche's naturalism
- about slave morality and *ressentiment*.

The overcoming of morality, or even (in a certain sense)
the self-overcoming of morality: let that be the name for
the long, clandestine work that was kept in reserve for the
most subtle and honest (and also the most malicious)
people of conscience today, living touchstones of the
human heart.

(*BGE*, 32)

Morality

Morality is the branch of philosophy that studies what is good
and what is right. It is usually studied from two different
perspectives: **normative ethics** and **meta-ethics**. Whereas
normative ethics is concerned with what sort of things are good
and in providing guidance for moral decision making, meta-
ethics (also referred to as analytic ethics) is primarily concerned
with what we *mean* when, for example, we say 'good' or 'bad'
or 'just', etc. For example, normative ethics may advise us on
whether or not it is morally good or bad to have an abortion. In
this respect, normative ethics can be seen as more concrete and
practical. Meta-ethics, however, is concerned with the language
we use, i.e. how do we *define* 'good' or 'bad' when we say
'abortion is good' or 'abortion is bad' and so, in this way, is of
a more abstract nature. However, just because it may be more
abstract does not mean it is any less important, and some
philosophers would argue that there is little point in looking for
guidance as to what is good without understanding what we
mean by using the term 'good'.

More specifically, meta-ethics attempts to answer such questions
as where do our morals come from? Are they a product of our
culture and history, or when we use the term 'good', for
example, are we in some way tapping into a universal goodness
that is a law of the universe in perhaps the same way as certain
mathematical laws appear to be? If it is the former then morality
is a subjective human invention, whereas if it is the latter then
humans can, theoretically at least, discover objective facts about
the universe. The distinction between normative and meta-ethics

is not always a clear one, and certainly many moral philosophers would not have made such a distinction. Whereas meta-ethics has been dominant in twentieth-century moral philosophy, especially in Britain and America, its origins actually rest with the beginning of philosophy proper and the work of Plato (and probably Socrates) some two-and-a-half thousand years ago. Therefore, there is nothing 'new' about meta-ethics apart from the terminology and a more sophisticated development.

Nietzsche is primarily concerned with meta-ethical issues and, in fact, is probably the most ruthless critic of the moral philosophical tradition that you will find. For example: 'Moral judgement belongs, as does religious judgement, to a level of ignorance at which even the concept of the real, the distinction between the real and imaginary is lacking.' (*TI*, VII.1). Nietzsche's morality permeates all of his works, but the most systematic works of moral philosophy are *Beyond Good and Evil* and its 'sequel' *The Genealogy of Morals*.

The death of God

Nietzsche is not so much concerned with the fact that our beliefs are false, but rather with the belief *about* these beliefs. That is, why should we hold the beliefs that we do? At the beginning of Nietzsche's epitome *Beyond Good and Evil*, he raises the question of why we want truth; why not *untruth*? It is frequently the career of philosophers to seek for truth, and Nietzsche targets them for his main criticism. He believed the most important question should not be what is true or not but the extent to which a belief supports life and maintains a species. When philosophers make claims to truth they are merely presenting a preconceived dogma that tells you more about the philosopher's beliefs than anything to do with truths. For Nietzsche, this is especially true in the case of moral philosophy; an attempt to make a science of morals, to establish an objective morality.

In *The Gay Science*, Nietzsche first declares that God is dead: 'God is dead. God remains dead. And we have killed him' (GS, 125). By this, Nietzsche means that society no longer has a use for God; the belief does not in any way help the survival of the species, rather it hinders. The implications of this are important for ethics, for with the death of God comes the death of religious, especially Christian, morality: a morality that has underpinned western culture since the fourth century.

Nietzsche's naturalism

Nietzsche's philosophy influenced two significant thinkers: the psychoanalyst Sigmund Freud (1856–1939) and the philosopher Michel Foucault (1926–84). Yet, as the Nietzsche scholar Brian Leiter has noted, these two thinkers interpret Nietzsche very differently. On the one hand, Freud saw Nietzsche as a philosopher who revealed deep, hidden *facts* about human nature that help to explain what we are, while, on the other hand, Foucault praises Nietzsche for denying that there are any facts about human nature! Which of these views is the more accurate understanding of Nietzsche?

The question is an important one in terms of his views on morality because so many moral philosophers previous to Nietzsche have attempted to establish a moral outlook on the belief that there are facts about human nature. The view that our morality can be based in some way on our nature is referred to as **ethical naturalism**. Famous philosophers who would be considered ethical naturalists include the British utilitarians Jeremy Bentham (1748–1832) and John Stuart Mill (1806–73), and also the German philosopher Immanuel Kant (1724–1804). However, naturalism has its origins with the Ancient Greeks, as so much of philosophy does: Aristotle (384–322 BC) could also be considered a naturalist in his ethics. As an example of how naturalism works, if we take Bentham's utilitarianism, it works on the principle that it is human nature to avoid pain and pursue pleasure. Given this supposed fact of human nature, Bentham argues that moral decisions should be based on the amount of pain and pleasure the act causes: the greater the amount of happiness, the more morally right the act. Kant, for his part, focussed on the rational element of human nature – rather than emotions – and on that basis argued that the best moral decisions are rational decisions. This is an all-too simplistic account of what are extremely complex ethical theories, but the point is that it is believed that if it can be determined what is fundamental about our human nature – what makes us 'tick' so to speak – then we have a sound psychological, semi-scientific basis for our actions.

The modern view regards Nietzsche also as an ethical naturalist as opposed to Foucault's conception of Nietzsche as denying that there are any facts about nature. It is the 'modern' view because scholarship regarding Nietzsche has changed over the years and certainly in the mid-twentieth century Nietzsche was considered more the champion of existentialism (see Chapter 10 for much more on this): existence preceded essence, we are what we make of ourselves and have no 'function' or 'purpose' aside from what we give. Whilst is it correct to say that there are existential characteristics of Nietzsche's philosophy, he is perhaps in other respects more of a traditionalist than people might have imagined, despite his 'God is dead' declaration.

We can say with certainty that Nietzsche opposes attempts to find moral truths in some transcendent metaphysics, such as that presented by Plato. Yet it seems curious that Nietzsche is both very critical of the moral philosophical tradition and yet at the same time seems very much a part of it, at least in the naturalist sense. He thinks that every moral system so far produced is naive and, in the case of utilitarianism, 'boneheaded'. Such extreme scepticism and malevolent language understandably suggest that Nietzsche has no time for attempts at moral systems, but when you read the following from *Beyond Good and Evil* the impression is different:

> For to return man to nature; to master the many conceited and gushing interpretations and secondary meanings that have heretofore been scribbled and painted

over that eternal original text *homo natura*; to ensure
that henceforth man faces man in the same way that
currently, grown tough with the discipline of science, he
faces the *other* nature ...'

(*BGE* 230)

The emphasis in commentaries is often placed on Nietzsche's
reference to the 'discipline of science' in the above and so it has
been argued that Nietzsche intends his moral philosophy to be
in line with scientific, empirical enquiry. However, while it is one
thing to say that metaphysical speculation should be rejected –
and this rejection seems a correct reading of Nietzsche – it may
be going too far to say that Nietzsche intended his moral
philosophy to be based upon scientific (and by 'scientific' here is
meant discoveries in human physiology and psychology
especially) discoveries. A more accurate reading of the quote
above is that Nietzsche wanted moral investigation to be *as
rigorous as* scientific method, not *a reflection of* scientific
discoveries. However, this reading is also somewhat
unsatisfactory because if we are not able to make any reference
to scientific facts about nature then it is difficult to see how
human beings can be 'translated back into nature'. At best, all
Nietzsche seems to be saying here is that we should avoid idle
metaphysical speculation and he often uses terms in his texts
such as 'observe better' and 'study more' which suggests we
need to be more disciplined and rigorous in our approach to
moral investigation in a way analogous to scientific method.

However, how we are to be 'more disciplined' is not altogether
clear and nor is it clear whether such attempts at scientific
rigour would produce positive results. If Nietzsche is simply
saying that we should copy scientific methods (in terms of
detecting cause and effect) of determining moral actions then it
could well be argued that other suspect disciplines, such as
astrology, for instance, are justified in their methods. An
astrologer looks for causes for actions: the fact that he or she
believes those causes is inherent within the alignment of stars is
irrelevant *unless* you want to argue that such claims must also
be supported by scientific *evidence*. Therefore, it is not just the

method that is important, but the results must also be continuous with the results of science. Only *then* can we say that astrology is 'bad science'. But as shall be shown in this chapter, Nietzsche makes a number of claims about morality (and other things such as the will to power) that have little or no basis in scientific or empirical evidence. As with his talk of the will to power (see Chapter 05) it seems that we have to see Nietzsche's moral philosophy as an attempt to get us to react, to present a psychological thesis rather than to argue for any factual account of morality, in which case Nietzsche does not seem to be a naturalist at all, and Foucault may well have been right in his interpretation!

The debate over the degree to which Nietzsche is an ethical naturalist or not is an ongoing one and requires a lot more close reading and debate than is available here.

More Challenging:

A Problem with Ethical Naturalism: The Naturalistic Fallacy

Another problem with ethical naturalism more generally, but which can also be specifically addressed towards Nietzsche if he is a naturalist, is that he could then be accused of what is known as the **naturalistic fallacy**. The Scottish empiricist philosopher David Hume (1711–76) famously wrote:

> In every system of morality, which I have hitherto met with, I have always remarked, that the author proceeds for some time in the ordinary way of reasoning, and establishes the being of God, or makes observations concerning human affairs; when of a sudden I am surprised to find, that instead of the usual copulations of propositions, is, and is not, I meet with no proposition that is not connected with an ought, or an ought not. This change is imperceptible; but is, however, of the last consequence. For as this ought, or ought not, expresses some new relation or affirmation, 'tis necessary that it should be observed and explained; and at the same time that a reason should be given, for what seems altogether

inconceivable, how this new relation can be a deduction from others, which are entirely different from it.

(*A Treatise of Human Nature*)

What Hume is suggesting here is that moral philosophers are responsible for an error in logic when they move from factual statement to value statements: from an 'is' (fact) to an 'ought' (value). For example, consider the following argument:

1. There are many poor people in the world.
2. The wealthy nations have the financial means to end world poverty.
3. Therefore, the wealthy nations *should* end world poverty.

Given the first two factual statements above, Hume observes that the conclusion does not logically follow. You could quite easily replace the conclusion with, for example, 'Therefore, the wealthy nations *should* get wealthier!' Whilst we may be morally outraged by this conclusion, there is nothing *logically necessary* in the statement that rich nations should help poor nations. For the argument to be logically necessary, it requires **deduction**, for example:

1. There are many poor people in the world.
2. John is poor.
3. Therefore, John is one of many poor people in the world.

This is a deductive argument because given the factual statements 1 and 2, then the factual statement 3 follows logically. Importantly here an 'ought' is not being introduced, just factual statements. The rightness or wrongness of the facts is not an issue here. If you consider utilitarianism again, of which Nietzsche was so critical:

1. Human beings *have* a given nature.
2. The nature of human beings *is* to avoid pain and pursue pleasure.
3. Therefore, human beings *ought* to avoid pain and pursue pleasure.

The first two statements are *factual* (although they could, of course, be wrong), but the third is a *value* statement. Hume brilliantly highlighted a crucial error here, that applies equally to Kant (we *are* rational, therefore we *ought to* be rational) and Aristotle (we *have* a function, therefore we *ought* to fulfil our function). If Nietzsche is also a naturalist then he can be accused of making the same logical error.

Slave morality

Two years after *Genealogy*, Nietzsche wrote *Ecce Homo* and there he states clearly the intention of the First Essay of *Genealogy*:

> The truth of the *first* inquiry is the birth of Christianity out of the spirit of *ressentiment*, not, as people may believe, out of the 'spirit' – a countermovement by its very nature, the great rebellion against the dominion of *noble* values.

> (*EH*, III)

In fact, Essay 1 is an elaboration of the relatively lengthy Section 260 of *Beyond Good and Evil*. The very title of the book with the use of the word 'genealogy' is important as it is provocative of the time to so much as suggest that morals *have* a genealogy, that is, a history and development, rather than adopting the view that morals are just 'there' waiting to be discovered. This, then, is Nietzsche's main argument of the whole text, but as stated in Essay 1: morals are not universal and immutable, but are historical products that are therefore contingent creations of particular people at particular times with particular *motives*. The emphasis on motives is important here, because where Nietzsche is particularly original is in getting us to question the value of our morals rather than to assume that moral values are intrinsically valuable. This enterprise is also indicated in the title *Beyond Good and Evil*: to understand what we mean when we use moral terms such as 'good' and 'evil' we need to go *beyond* them. In addition, Nietzsche thinks moral philosophers are wrong in believing that modern man is morally better than past generations and he especially attacks utilitarianism which was the dominant moral theory at the time. The fact that Nietzsche claims that our morality has a traceable evolved ancestry at all would have shocked many a reader in his time, for morals were seen as given by the divine lawgiver God and so there is no genealogy to trace. If the lawgiver disappears, then so does the law and the fear that what will result will be moral anarchy. Yet Nietzsche argues that morality can be explained in naturalistic terms, without the need for a God or gods. They are natural phenomena that have evolved as a result of the need to keep societies together and to check instinctual drives that would destroy the unity of the group if they were allowed free reign. Therefore, morality is a result of circumstance, and it is the circumstance that comes first which is then followed by morality, not the other way around.

For Nietzsche, morality:

• is a result of circumstance, not the other way around
• serves a useful function in that it binds the fabric of the group
• can, however, outlive its use and become a hindering custom.

If morality ceases to serve a useful function, yet continues to be maintained by society, then this might stunt the growth of that society because we continue to live by rules that are no longer applicable to contemporary society. Nietzsche looked to his own society and saw it to be in a state of decay for this very reason, i.e. that it looks to the old values; the old *Christian* values. When Nietzsche talks of the morality of Western Europe as being the product of a particular time and people, what he had in mind in terms of the people were Christian slaves and at the time and place of the Roman Empire *circa* the first to the third centuries AD. This is why he refers to morality of his time as 'slave morality' as opposed to the 'noble' morality possessed by the Romans before the coming of Christianity. What is needed is a *new morality*. By considering the genealogy of morals Nietzsche hoped to demonstrate why we have the values we do. This way, if we still continue to hold such values, we are at least aware that they are effectively redundant. Nietzsche's ultimate hope is that we, or perhaps the Superman (see Chapter 06), will create new values.

In considering why Christianity originates with the slaves of the Roman Empire, Nietzsche argued that they saw this as a way of release from bondage. As the slaves were not powerful enough to literally free themselves from their masters, they were consoled by religious belief that provided them with spiritual liberation. Christianity, like everything else, is an expression of the will to power. The first Christians were slaves under the Roman Empire and so the only way they could assert any kind of superiority over the Romans was to assume a higher spiritual status. This was achieved, according to Nietzsche, by inverting the values of society. For example, values such as compassion or pity were regarded by Christians as righteous values that would lead to reward from God, whereas other values such as self-interest were seen as sinful.

Nietzsche argued that the expression of pity is a weapon the weak use against the strong. Nietzsche criticized the view of pity presented by Schopenhauer and Wagner who believed that when you feel pity you experience their suffering as if it were your own for, at the bottom of Schopenhauer's Will, we are all identical beings. Nietzsche, however, did not believe it was possible to literally feel someone else's pain and, therefore, experience 'true pity'. To want pity is to want others to suffer with you. Nietzsche observed that the effort of some neurotics to arouse pity in others is because they wish to hurt others and to demonstrate that they at least have this power.

Ressentiment

The real motive for promoting such values was not because there actually is a God that enforces such values, but because the slaves resented the status of the Romans and wanted to possess their power. This is what Nietzsche means by the French term *ressentiment*. The slave feels relatively impotent compared with the master and he is not able to accept the idea that he is treated worse than others. This leads to hostility, to resentment, yet he is unable to release this hostility because of his enslavement. What is the slave to do? He cannot simply use brute force, as this will result in him being in a worse state than before, and so he must use *guile*.

In order to enact revenge upon his master, the slave uses the weapon of moral conduct. It consists of getting the master to acquiesce to the moral code of the slave and, as a result, appraise himself according to the slave's perspective. As Christians, of course, the slaves should not have the option of revenge, for they should 'turn the other cheek'. However, so successful were the slaves in their guile and secrecy that they managed to disguise their revenge under the cloak of pure intentions.

As the master estimates his own worth according to the values of the slave, he will perceive himself and his actions as evil and reprehensible. His old aristocratic values will be discarded, as he feels morally obliged to do 'good' in the Christian sense. Nietzsche portrays the Roman aristocrat as physically powerful, healthy and aggressive. These qualities remain but, unable to express them internally, they are directed inwards. The aristocrat ends up punishing himself rather than others.

For Nietzsche, slave morality could only have arisen out of hatred and fear. The slave's morality is a reaction to the actions of others. That is, when someone does something to you that you resent, then you class it as 'bad' and, consequently, you create a morality in opposition to this: that is 'good'. If you are frightened of your neighbour you react by wanting your neighbour to love you and this is why love is a Christian virtue. The master's morality, however, is not a reaction to others at all. The master has no need to view himself according to the actions of others, but rather affirms himself. He does not require to be loved or for everyone to conform. The master can also hate, but this hatred is discharged in a 'healthy' manner through direct action, rather than, in the case of the weak, through resentment.

Nietzsche is presenting both an historical and psychological portrayal, and it is dubious on both counts. From the psychological point of view, Nietzsche portrays the slave as someone with so much pent-up aggression that it becomes poisonous unless it is expressed in some 'natural' way. This resembles the equally unconvincing psychological theory that children should be allowed to let out their aggression otherwise it will remain bottled up inside and express itself in later life in some other form. From the historical perspective we must allow Nietzsche a certain degree of artistic licence so long as the point is made. He is specifically thinking of Christianity when he talks of religion. Nietzsche was not talking about all religions, for he admired the Greek religion. His main concern with Christianity was its dehumanization: because God is regarded so highly, as perfect and all-good in fact, then it logically follows that man regards himself so lowly, as necessarily imperfect and sinful. Nietzsche did also criticize Jewish slave-morality for being the originator of Christian morality.

One of the misunderstandings of Nietzsche's philosophy needs to be made clear at this point. Nietzsche was not an anti-Semite. It is clear from his correspondence that he hated anti-Semites and, in fact, all racist theories. This misunderstanding derives from reading Nietzsche out of context, always a dangerous thing to do, as well as Nietzsche's youthful enthusiasm for Wagner's ideas, and Wagner most definitely was an anti-Semite. Nietzsche's sister Elisabeth, who married an anti-Semite, interpreted her brother's works as anti-Jewish. Nietzsche's language can be easily misinterpreted, especially when he uses such phrases as 'blond beast' (GM, 11) when referring to the masters. This has been used as an indication that Nietzsche supported German nationalism and Hitler's views on Aryanism. However, what Nietzsche actually meant by 'blond beast' was a reference to the lion as king of the beasts.

Nonetheless, Nietzsche's views on the master-slave morality are perhaps his most controversial and it is easy to understand why this is the case when a few of the main points are considered:

- The master morality made a distinction between 'good' and 'bad'. 'Good' applies to those who are united, noble and strong. 'Bad' refers to the slaves who are weak and base.
- This notion of 'good' and 'bad' therefore is *not* moral. 'Bad' merely meant to be one of the herd, the 'low-minded'. 'Good' meant the noble and intellectual.
- Christianity reinterpreted 'good' and 'bad' as 'good' and 'evil'. 'Good' was now represented by the life and teaching of Jesus Christ; such values as altruism. 'Evil' became what for the masters was previously 'good'.

Nietzsche obviously admires the 'masters' and there is a certain pro-aristocracy element to him here. Nietzsche evidently approves of a firmly defined class structure and had a disdain for the moral and social mores of the masses. He was certainly very conservative in this respect and was no liberal democrat (see Chapter 09 for his political views).

The priests

Nietzsche specifically attacks the Christian priests in their role of promoting the slave morality. The priests were in the unique position in society in that they were both strong and weak at the same time. They were weak in relation to the aristocratic masters, but they were strong spiritually because they were God's agents on earth. The pastoral, as opposed to the royal, power that the priests possessed was used as a tool for social control and promoting the moral ideal of the herd.

Although he refers to the herd, or slave, morality as promoting the teachings of Christ, Nietzsche places the blame firmly on St Paul as the one who misinterpreted Jesus' teachings. In fact, Nietzsche regards Jesus as a member of the master morality because Jesus was a life affirmer who criticized the Jewish priests for using religion as a means of social control. St Paul, who travelled across the Roman Empire establishing churches in the first century, set the stage for the development of the slave morality and corrupted Jesus' teachings to suit his own ends. The ethic that was endorsed was one of asceticism and self-denial. St Paul was a Roman citizen and was educated in Greek philosophy and so he made Christianity acceptable to the Romans by incorporating Greek philosophical ideas, especially the Platonic view of dualism. An outlook was presented based on a dualistic worldview: this world being one of necessary suffering, but preparation for a better world in the next life. This world was inferior, therefore, to the next world and the priests had turned Christianity into life denying, instead of Christ's life affirmation.

The revaluation of all values

For Nietzsche, the declaration that 'God is dead' sets man free to become his/her own being, to be the 'Superman'. Their morality is a rejection of the herd morality. These are the elite; people who have mastered their own will to power and created life-affirming values to live by. The most crucial value for Nietzsche was that we should be life affirming. The Superman, therefore, is one who realizes the potential of being a human being and is not consoled by a belief in the next life. The Superman has mastered himself and creates his own values.

The practical implications of his philosophy are not something Nietzsche gave much consideration to. Nietzsche is not a democratic philosopher, for he is not a supporter of the values of the common herd. He believed in the great man, the hero, the Superman, who should be a law unto himself. However, it is difficult to see how a society that consisted of such an elite that establishes its own values would function in society. They would, presumably, look towards the masses with contempt and one wonders how the Superman could live either amongst the masses or even amongst themselves. There would be inevitable conflict, although Nietzsche would have welcomed this provided it led to a revaluation of values.

Nietzsche's rejection of such Christian values as turning the other cheek, loving your neighbour and compassion for those that are suffering, might come across as somewhat callous. For one reason or another, many are unable to stand on their own two feet or face the realities of life and so there is a need for compassion. However, Nietzsche did not despise such values as compassion; rather it is the use of it as a psychological prop instead of looking towards one's own resources. Nietzsche's own almost crippling illness plagued him for most of his life, but the last thing he would have wanted was compassion or pity.

However, Nietzsche seems too selective when talking about religion (see Chapter 08 for more on Nietzsche's religious views), asserting the negative while ignoring the variety of religious belief. Even if it were the case that Christianity is the cause of a slave morality, it has also been a vehicle of many revolutionary changes that Nietzsche himself might approve of. The same can be said of many other religions that Nietzsche would regard as 'life denying'. Where does Nietzsche get *his* values? Nietzsche does not envisage his Superman as someone who is mean, vindictive or indiscriminately violent and cruel. Yet we must wonder why this Superman should not be violent and cruel? How can Nietzsche pick and choose the Superman's morality? Perhaps Nietzsche himself did not fully escape the values of his own religious upbringing.

Summary

- Nietzsche's main concern was not whether beliefs are true or false, but why we believe what we do.
- Nietzsche's moral philosophy is a form of ethical naturalism.
- He presents a genealogy of Christian morality, tracing it to the slaves of the Roman Empire.
- Christian morality is an expression of the will to power. Its values are based on the slaves' *ressentiment* towards their masters.
- The most important values, for Nietzsche, are those that affirm life. His criticism of Christian morality is that it rejects life and is based on hatred and fear.

05

the will to power

In this chapter you will learn:
- how important the will to power is for Nietzsche's philosophy
- to what extent the will to power can be seen as an explanation for how the world works
- to what extent the will to power can be seen as a subjective phenomenon
- a possible third explanation of the will to power as providing an empirical account of the world.

What is the will to power?

As discussed below, the debate over what the will to power actually *is* and how much importance should be attached to it centres on two differing interpretations:

1. **An objective explanation for everything.** Nietzsche wants to give us a metaphysical picture of the world – a 'theory of everything' that explains the world of experience but, nonetheless, is 'beyond' the physical (hence 'metaphysical').
2. **A subjective interpretation.** This is not asserting that there is a world 'out there' beyond the physical, but is simply putting forward the will to power as a subjective interpretation.

Both these interpretations will be considered as well as a possible third interpretation, but first it will help to speculate on why there exists such diverse understandings and how much importance should be attributed to this doctrine.

The enigma of the will to power

The will to power is certainly one of the most famous contributions that Nietzsche made to philosophy, yet it is also a concept that is subject to a variety of differing interpretations by scholars. Nietzsche, for his part, is not always helpful in his own articulation of the will to power either, which inevitably opens him up to speculation and disagreement amongst his readers. Much writing on the will to power, especially early scholarship, places this concept at the heart of Nietzsche's philosophy, as the underlying concept for all of his philosophical views on such things as morality, art and nature. More recent scholarship, however, has raised questions as to whether Nietzsche really gives us a strong doctrine of the will to power *at all*.

Has the importance of the will to power for Nietzsche's philosophy been over-played? It is certainly curious that Nietzsche seemed to 'drop' any reference to the will to power in his last major work, *Ecce Homo*. This omission is significant because in this work Nietzsche reflects upon his ideas in all his previous works. To make no mention of the will to power at all certainly suggests that he no longer considered it important. In addition, in 1886, Nietzsche wrote a series of new prefaces to *The Birth of Tragedy*, *Human, All Too Human*, *Daybreak* and *The Gay Science* in which he reflected upon his major philosophical themes, yet the will to power was again not mentioned.

However, although he may have decided against developing the will to power in his published works, this is not to say that it was not a doctrine that ceased to preoccupy him – quite the opposite, in fact. The reason Nietzsche wrote new prefaces for many of his earlier books was because he was in the process of changing publishers as he had learnt that his old publisher had two-thirds of his books stuffed in a warehouse with little attempt to push sales. After writing books for 15 years, it would have been a huge disappointment to Nietzsche to discover that his publisher had made little effort to sell his books. By launching with a new publisher, Nietzsche hoped for a fresh beginning and so wrote a series of new prefaces. He also decided to start a new work with the title *The Will to Power: Attempt at a New Interpretation of Everything that Happens*. The title alone is quite revealing and does suggest that Nietzsche believed in at least the *possibility* of the will to power as an important contribution to his philosophical enterprise. This project became almost an obsession (and certainly a therapeutic aid against depression) for Nietzsche and, for that reason if for no other, it should not be surprising that his sister and Peter Gast should collect his notes together into a work with the title *will to power*. Nietzsche's project was intended to be a major four-volume work that would have a coherent structure unlike his previous collections of aphorisms and short essays. However, in the autumn of 1888, he completed *The Antichrist* which was intended to be the first volume of his great work, yet ended up being the whole work itself. Nietzsche had previously given up on the title 'will to power' anyway and was leaning towards 'Revaluation of All Values' which, in retrospect, seems more fitting to his life-long enterprise. Hence he wrote, 'My revaluation of all values, which has *The Antichrist* as its main title, is finished.'

It is, then, perhaps going too far to say that Nietzsche places *no* importance on the will to power. The terms 'will to power' and 'power' are used explicitly throughout many of his works, as well as implicitly. The fact also that Nietzsche was so preoccupied with it through much of his sane life suggests it has some value, even if Nietzsche saw it more as a tentative experiment rather than a fully worked-out doctrine.

Two important passages on the will to power

Quote from *The Will to Power*:

And do you know what 'the world' is to me? Shall I show it to you in my mirror? This world: a monster of energy, without beginning, without end; a firm, iron magnitude of force that does not grow bigger or smaller, that does not expend itself but only transforms itself; as a whole of unalterable size, a household without expenses or losses, but likewise without increase or income; enclosed by 'nothingness' as by a boundary; not something blurry or wasted, not something endlessly extended, but set in a definite space as a definite force, and not a space that might be 'empty' here or there, but rather as a force throughout, as a play of forces and waves of forces [...] do you want a *name* for this world? A *solution* for all its riddles? A *light* for you, too, you best-concealed, strongest, most intrepid, most midnightly men? – *This world is the will to power – and nothing besides!* And you yourselves are also this will to power – and nothing besides!

(*The Will to Power* 1067)

Quote from *Beyond Good and Evil*:

Assuming, finally, that we could explain our entire instinctual life as the development and differentiation of *one* basic form of the will (namely the will to power, as my tenet would have it); assuming that one could derive all organic functions from this will to power and also find in it the solution of the problem of procreation and alimentation (it is all one problem), then we would have won the right to designate *all* effective energy unequivocally as: the *will to power*. The world as it is seen from the inside, the world defined and described by its 'intelligible character' – would be simply 'will to power' and that alone.

(*BGE*, 36)

First interpretation: An objective explanation for everything

The *traditional* view looks to the will to power as an explanation for all of life's manifestations. It is a neutral 'force' that governs the world that is akin to Schopenhauer's concept of the will that was considered in Chapter 02. The best way to understand this view of the will to power is to look at the first quote from the collected notes *The Will to Power* in the box opposite.

This passage has its attractions in its picture of the world as a 'monster of energy' and seems to point to a belief on Nietzsche's part in some underlying principle, a 'theory of everything'. To support this interpretation, some scholars would cite the importance of the pre-Socratics for Nietzsche who, on the whole, were distinguished by the belief that there is an underlying principle that governs the universe, an *archê* (first principle) that is the origin of and responsible for all things. For example, the Greek philosopher Thales (circa 625–545 BC) presented a form of **material monism**: that the universe consists ultimately of only one substance. What makes Thales stand out here was to pronounce that there are fundamental features of the universe that are not immediately accessible to the senses or to 'common sense'. It makes us think that the world is not as it at first seems: there are inner workings to be uncovered. Thales was not so concerned with the Homeric gods at play, but adopted a materialist view that all things were made of material substance and it is possible to uncover patterns and laws for this material stuff. Thales, in his case, concluded that the seeming multiplicity of the universe can be reduced to the fundamental substance of water which, of course, is wrong, but at least he began the philosophical enterprise of seeking an underlying explanation for all things.

Is this, then, what Nietzsche's doctrine of the will to power is? A view of the underlying principles of the universe as a multiplicity of drives seeking power over one another? This may be one possible understanding which can be explored some more in this chapter, but we need to be aware that things are not that simple. Taken at face value this much-quoted passage certainly seems to assert that the will to power is an all-encompassing phenomenon; the very essence of life itself, '*This world is the will to power – and nothing besides!*' But we need to be very careful of our sources when reading Nietzsche. The above quote is from section 1067 of *will to power* which, as already mentioned, is a work that has been much discredited as it is really a compilation of Nietzsche's notes edited by his sister who had her own political and ideological agenda. In fact, Nietzsche himself had discarded the passage in 1887, and so he would not have endorsed its publication, thus giving it a printed status it does not deserve.

We must look to works that Nietzsche wished to be published to see if a 'theory of everything' thesis can be supported. Interestingly, Nietzsche, throughout the whole of his works, only presents *one* argument (if 'argument' is the right word here) for the will to power. This is contained in Section 36 of *Beyond Good and Evil* which is the second quote in the box above.

Does this really differ that much from the quote from the *will to power* earlier? In very subtle ways it does, but the subtlety – in Nietzsche's case – is always important. Nietzsche was a trained philologist, remember, and he chose his words carefully. If you read *The Will to Power* passage again you will note how assertive it is, how certain; but these were notes and not intended to be published. When it actually comes to writing something for intended publication, Nietzsche is more circumspect in his choice of words, more cautious. For example, he starts off with the word 'Assuming' and then uses words such as 'if' followed by 'then'. The important point that Nietzsche is trying to get across is that we should not remain silent or be sceptical on such topics, but that we should realize that when we attempt to contemplate metaphysical 'truths' we are confronted with the problem of how to actually understand 'truth'. This is a puzzle, a conundrum, a riddle that Nietzsche is very fond of. When scholars interpret Nietzsche they sometimes forget the importance he places on the use of language, as well as his own playfulness with words and with his expertise in the Ancient Greek tradition of irony. By using such terms as 'intelligible character' – put into inverted commas by Nietzsche – he is making a reference to Kant and his belief in the world 'in itself', but Nietzsche himself does not assert that there is a world 'in itself' a noumenal world separate from the world of appearance. Rather, *supposing* it would be possible for there to be a world 'in itself' it would actually be no different from the world of appearance.

Whereas Nietzsche's earlier writings may suggest a view of the will to power as akin to Schopenhauer's will to life, as an explanation for all phenomena, the essence to life itself, by the time of his more mature work – and in particular in his 'trilogy' of *Thus Spoke Zarathustra*, *Beyond Good and Evil* and *The Genealogy of Morals*, Nietzsche had seemingly rejected this view. Consider this passage from *Thus Spoke Zarathustra*:

> He who shot the doctrine of 'will to existence' at truth certainly did not hit the truth: this will – does not exist! Only where life is, there is also will: not will to life, but – so I teach you – will to power! The living creature values many things higher than life itself; yet out of this evaluation itself speaks – the will to power! Thus life once taught me: and with this teaching do I solve the riddle of your hearts, you wisest men.

> *(TSZ II. 12)*

Here Nietzsche is rejecting Schopenhauer's metaphysical doctrine of the will, and so it would be surprising if the replacement of this with the will to power is also meant to be metaphysical, in which case how would it differ *at all* from Schopenhauer? Also, in his mature work, Nietzsche is explicit – as much as he ever is explicit – in his rejection of metaphysical speculation. For example, in his Preface of *Beyond Good and Evil* he considers such 'philosophical dogmatism' to be 'some folk superstition from time immemorial ... some play on words perhaps, some seductive aspect of grammar, or a daring generalization from very limited, very personal, very human, all-too-human facts' and then, in Section One, he considers a belief in metaphysical truths as the 'prejudice' of philosophers. Or consider the title of one section of *The Twilight of the Idols*: 'How the Real World Finally Became a Fable'. With such explicit attacks on metaphysics it is certainly difficult to sustain a view that Nietzsche's will to power is metaphysical in character.

Those scholars who have attempted to argue that Nietzsche's will to power is a reference to the underlying 'substance' of the world, to the world as a 'monster of energy, without beginning, without end' (*WP*, 1067) have had to rely mostly upon the discredited work *The Will to Power* as their source. Attractive though this concept of the will to power may be, it does not hold up to scrutiny when seen in the light of works that Nietzsche *intended* to have published. In fact, to suggest that Nietzsche wanted to put forward a 'theory of everything' may well go against what he stood for. For example, when we read what Nietzsche said in *Beyond Good and Evil*:

> ... what formerly happened with the Stoics still happens today, too, as soon as any philosophy begins to believe in itself. It always creates the world in its own image.
>
> (*BGE* 9)

This passage can be read in a number of ways: on the one hand he is accusing the Stoics of imposing a particular view upon nature but, on the other, Nietzsche seems to be suggesting this is something that philosophy *inevitably does*. Whilst he may be criticizing the Stoics for 'creating the world in its own image' he seems to be admitting that this is unavoidable. Therefore, is Nietzsche acknowledging that his speculations on the will to power are an assertion of some underlying fact about nature whilst also being aware that any assertions, any statements of 'facts', are ultimately the philosopher's own prejudices? Such ambiguities are typical of Nietzsche and there is certainly a tension between Nietzsche speaking of nature in terms of universal, natural laws, and his constant warning against engaging in such metaphysical speculation.

Second interpretation: A subjective interpretation

Passage suggesting the will to power is just one interpretation

... somebody with an opposite intention and mode of interpretation could come along and be able to read from nature, and with reference to the same set of appearances, a tyrannically ruthless and pitiless execution of power claims. This sort of interpreter would show the unequivocal and unconditional nature of all 'will to power' so vividly and graphically that almost every word, and even the word 'tyranny', would ultimately seem useless [...] Granted, this is only an interpretation too – and you will be eager enough to make this objection? – well then, so much the better.

(*BGE* 22)

The final sentence of the quote above is particularly instructive as it appears to be an admission that his talk of the will to power is his *own* interpretation and is therefore no 'truer' than that put forward by any other philosopher. But if it is indeed the case that the will to power is no more true than any other view of the world, and if Nietzsche knows he is putting forward his own subjective view, then why give it any credence? To answer this it is important to remember how much value needs to be placed on Nietzsche's style: on his use of metaphor, ambiguity, riddles, humour and irony. Nietzsche knows he is seeing the world from his own perspective, for how can he – or anybody else for that matter – do otherwise? Nonetheless, the knowledge that one cannot demonstrate objective truths, that one cannot step outside of one's own perspective, is not a reason to then remain silent or to adopt a nihilistic stance towards our values. Nietzsche, remember, is very positive; he does not bury his head in despair and existential nausea (although he has his moments), but rejoices with the realization that we cannot know what is true. Nietzsche, however, does not stop using words such as 'truth', 'soul', etc, but these words for Nietzsche mean something different. He writes about the will to power because *he* values it, not because it necessarily exists 'out there'.

Such a reading of Nietzsche is inevitably problematic as we are then faced with the dilemma of when, if ever, he is not talking metaphorically. Are we to say that all of his philosophy – his views on slave morality, the Superman, on tragedy, etc. – is his own prejudice; that there are no genuine truth-claims in any of his writings at all? If we accept this is the case then it does not necessarily follow that we should reject Nietzsche's writings, any more than we should reject anyone else's writings on the basis that they are 'value-preferences'.

The importance of a doctrine, of a teaching, lies here with the *reader*: Nietzsche often said that he was addressing a small audience, a 'select few' (although he was not so lacking in vanity as to not wish that more people bought his books) and so, provided they found something appealing in his writings, then he has succeeded. Novels, the best novels anyway, tend to reveal something about the world or/and about human nature, and the same can be said about many religious texts, whether you believe in the truth claims of religion or not. The Bible, for example, can be read on many levels; at one level the reader may read it from an 'anti-realist' stance, that is rejecting the theological claims that there is a God, or that Jesus is the son of God, while still reading the book as revealing 'truths' about human beings, their motives, drives, and so on. It is therefore perhaps not that surprising that Nietzsche often writes in poetical, literary and – certainly in the case of *Thus Spoke Zarathustra* – in a biblical manner, frequently resorting to parables. 'Truths' are revealed at the psychological level. That is to say, the will to power tells us a lot about how human beings – and possibly other organic species – interact with one another, what motivates them, and may well help to explain the origin of our beliefs and values. In that sense, Nietzsche's writings are a valuable contribution to knowledge.

If we see Nietzsche's views as a subjective interpretation that some of his readers can relate to, then what does it reveal concerning the nature of the will to power? It will help if it can be determined what Nietzsche is *not* saying: We are not, for example, striving for power *all* of the time. That would entail that when we are sleeping we are striving for power, or that every activity – however seemingly pointless – is an expression of the will to power. In addition, we are not always motivated by power. For example, watching a programme on TV or sightseeing in Paris does not seem to have any power-motivation behind it, although, in given circumstances, presumably it can be. The will to power, rather, is one drive amongst many, albeit an important one.

Given the importance of language and communication for Nietzsche, it seems appropriate to look to *Thus Spoke Zarathustra* as it is here where we can find Nietzsche's more systematic elaboration of the will to power as interpretation. In the Second Part of *Thus Spoke Zarathustra* – the chapter entitled 'Of Self-Overcoming' – Zarathustra declares: 'Where I found a living creature, there I found will to power.' The importance of the title of this chapter in his elaboration of the will to power should not be overlooked: of *self*-overcoming, or *self*-transcendence. Rather than seeing the will to power as some underlying principle of the world, it is seen first and foremost as the power over one's *self*. Reading the story of Zarathustra we have a character in the process of creation: creation of a new kind of world with new values. In this sense, Zarathustra can be seen as mirroring Nietzsche's own philosophical enterprise. When faced with a world that no longer had meaning or credibility in his eyes (and, Nietzsche believed, in the eyes of a select others, though growing in number he thought) he creates a world that does have meaning for him. Again, the issue of whether it is 'true' or not is something of an irrelevancy or, at best, merely highlighting the whole problem of trying to look at the world in polar opposites of 'true' or 'false'. Nietzsche often saw his Supermen as creative artists, painters and musicians and so the importance of creating a world for oneself that has value is a philosophical and artistic enterprise.

Related to this self-overcoming is self-enhancement. Whilst we can possibly survive with a world that lacks meaning, Nietzsche questions whether such a life is worth living. Self-preservation is one thing, but self-enhancement – the bettering of one's self – is another. In fact, mere self-preservation will inevitably lead to decay and destruction, whereas enhancement ensures we survive, and survive as better human beings. The will to power is when we say 'yes' to life and go on the offensive against mediocrity and what Nietzsche saw as decadent values. Nietzsche's first exploration into the will to power has its origins in *The Birth of Tragedy* when he talks of the interaction of the Dionysian and Apollonian artistic life forces (see Chapter 03). An expression of the will to power is to make sense of the world, to give it meaning, for, by making sense of the world, mankind overpowers it and brings it into a form that is in accordance with the self. The world reflects the self and the self recognizes his/her role within the world. Nietzsche saw this as a dangerous enterprise – life threatening and sanity threatening – because most people, Nietzsche believed, prefer to live 'herd-like' and unthinking rather than confront one's place in the world.

What is understood by 'truth', then, is whatever overcomes the world, whatever view of the world prevails. Truth is a mental construct; it is what is psychologically bearable. Early on in *Thus Spoke Zarathustra*, the prophet – rather naively it turns out – says the following: 'To lure many away from the herd – that is why I have come. The people and the herd shall be angry with me: the herdsmen shall call Zarathustra a robber' (*TSZ* I.9). In many ways, the mission of Zarathustra – and that of Nietzsche too – is like that of Socrates as Plato pictured him in his famous analogy of the cave. Briefly, in this analogy there are prisoners tied together at the bottom of the cave and who are brought up throughout their lives staring at shadows on the wall. The prisoners take these shadows to be reality until one day a prisoner is released and exits the cave. The released prisoner is then 'enlightened' to what the world is really like and feels duty-bound to return to the bottom of the cave and free his fellow prisoners. Plato uses this analogy to illustrate the role of the philosopher, and the freed prisoner can be seen as embodied in the character of Socrates who saw it his duty to go amongst the people of Athens and to question their deeply set values. Zarathustra saw his role in a similar manner, but the key difference between Socrates and Zarathustra (or, more accurately, between Plato and Nietzsche) is that the former saw 'truth' in a metaphysical way, whereas the latter saw 'truth' as a subjective, psychological phenomenon: it is a turning into one's self, rather than gazing at the stars above.

A third interpretation: the will to power as empirically true

To recap, so far two possible interpretations have been presented:

1. The will to power as presenting an objective metaphysical picture of the world.
2. The will to power as a subjective interpretation of the world that has psychological implications.

However, a third interpretation is that although Nietzsche did not intend to propose the will to power as metaphysical, he nonetheless wanted to say that it is something *much more than* merely subjective. That is, he wanted to present it as an empirical, scientific explanation of the *physical world* without any reference to a metaphysical world: our experience tells us that the world can be explained by the will to power. Through our senses and our observations of nature and how it operates, is it possible to explain its goings on as will to power and nothing else? This seems much more scientific than speculative, in the same way some scientists today look for a 'theory of everything'. Also, Nietzsche was not so anti-science, and could be quite positive about the role of science generally.

This view that the world, or at least the organic (which does, of course, also include human) world is will to power has been labelled the 'cosmological' doctrine of the will to power by the scholar Maudemarie Clark, although Clark goes on to say that Nietzsche does not actually present us with a cosmological doctrine at all. However, some would argue, the passage from Section 36 of *Beyond Good and Evil* quoted above (page 74) does seem to suggest at least a biological conception of the will to power. In one part of Section 36 Nietzsche says, 'all mechanical events, in so far as energy is active in them, are really the energy of the will, the effect of the will' and in the previous paragraph in the same section he talks about 'organic processes' in a similar manner. Given this, is Clark right to deny the cosmological view?

We need to consider what kind of picture the 'cosmos' would be if we were to say it is the 'will to power'? As a possible analogy which has been used, in the same way the state is made up of a collection of individuals, the world is made up of a collection of 'wills'. This form of analogy was not an uncommon one in Nietzsche's day as while sociologists saw society as an organism, biologists compared the organism to how society functions, and Nietzsche certainly liked reading the contemporary theories of biologists, zoologists, embryologists, physiologists and the like. It is nonetheless difficult to picture Nietzsche's world, despite the use of analogy. One scientist whom Nietzsche was all-too-familiar with is Charles Darwin, and at least one scholar has suggested that Nietzsche's world is Darwinian: the will to power as a product of natural selection whereby the world is made up of components fighting for dominance over one another. However, it is still unclear what these 'components' are. What, in other words, does Nietzsche mean by the will? Is the biological world made up of lots of 'little wills' striving for dominance and, if this is the case, do these wills have any sense of self-awareness?

To begin with, it does not seem to fit with Nietzsche's views on the self, the ego, to suggest that the will involves someone or something *willing*. For example, the French philosopher René Descartes (1596–1650) argued famously for a self in his expression: 'I think, therefore I am.' In other words, for there to be thoughts there must be a thinker. Similarly, for there to be will, there must be a subject doing the willing. In this sense, 'will' can be equated with 'desire'. But Nietzsche clearly rejects the idea of a self at all; he does not accept the seemingly logical consequence that a thought requires a thinker and therefore his talk of 'will' need not be seen in terms of subjects desiring something. 'Will' is not a conscious thing but is much more abstract and perhaps a better term for it is *drives*, for which *one* of those drives is the drive for power. Other drives may, for example, include the sexual drive, survival drive, pleasure drive and so on. The drive for power over others can in one way be seen as a separate drive, but also it could be seen as that which is common to all drives, for all kinds of drives 'want' to dominate over other drives. The world, then, is seen as a collection of organisms with distinctive drives that compete against each other for dominance. The human being, likewise, is seen as composed of a collection of competing drives.

The picture of the world as a bundle of organisms striving for power over one another may have its advocates, but it nonetheless leaves it open to speculation and a series of unanswered questions. If nothing else, it seems a rather simplistic and naïve picture that is neither philosophical nor particularly empirical. Are there really any grounds to suggest that every action in the world, every event, every cause and effect has as its impetus in the will to power in the sense Nietzsche seems to suggest? Fortunately, various passages in Nietzsche's works suggest that he did not consider that the world was 'will to power and nothings besides'. For example, take the following passage from *The Antichrist*:

> Life itself is to my mind the instinct for growth, for durability, for an accumulation of forces, for power: where the will to power is lacking there is decline. It is my contention that all the supreme values of mankind *lack* this will.
>
> (*AC* 6)

The passage is enlightening because, on the one hand, Nietzsche says that life itself is the instinct for power, but also states that the will to power can be 'lacking'. If something is *lacking* the will to power, then it does not make sense to say that everything *is* the will to power. In the same way, one molecule of water *is* two hydrogen atoms covalently bonded to a single oxygen atom. If you then say that one molecule is *lacking* an oxygen atom, then it makes little sense to still call it 'water'. Indeed, there are a number of other references in Nietzsche's works that suggest that the will to power is not the one underlying substance of the world, but rather one characteristic of the universe amongst others (such as desires, effects and so on).

Concluding remarks

Is the subjective understanding of the will to power the most accurate account of this enigma? Whilst a metaphysical understanding of the will to power seems way off the mark given what Nietzsche has to say about metaphysics and those philosophers who subscribe to a world 'out there', we also need to be cautious in arguing that Nietzsche was entirely proposing a subjective, psychological account. His eagerness to devour the writings of his contemporary theorizers in the realms of biology, physiology, embryology and the like, points to a certain degree of empathy for their views. Nietzsche at times can come across as strongly empirical and it would not be too far-fetched to suggest that, although he emphasized the subjective account of the will to power above all else, he ambitiously hoped – perhaps vainly – to underpin it in an empirical account of how the world *actually* seemed to operate.

Summary

• Although Nietzsche never gives us a systematic account of his will to power in his published writings, it would be inaccurate to say that it is therefore unimportant.

• The more traditional 'metaphysical' conception of the will to power seems less credible. Certainly, the metaphysical view goes against Nietzsche's own critical views on metaphysics.

• The will to power as a subjective account by Nietzsche has greater credibility amongst modern scholars, although perhaps Nietzsche did not entirely reject the view that it also provides an empirical account.

06

Zarathustra, the Superman and the eternal recurrence

In this chapter you will learn:
- about the story of *Thus Spoke Zarathustra*
- what Nietzsche meant by the 'Superman' (*Übermensch*)
- about the eternal recurrence
- about Nietzsche's views on nihilism
- about *amor fati*.

My formula for greatness in a human being is *amor fati*: that one wants nothing to be other than it is, not in the future, not in the past, not in all eternity.

(*EH*, Why I Am So Clever)

Thus Spoke Zarathustra

Although not his best philosophical work, *Thus Spoke Zarathustra* is Nietzsche's most widely-read book. In many respects, the foundations for that book can be found in *Human, all too Human* and *Dawn*, especially in the introduction of the concept of the will to power (see Chapter 05). In 1882 *The Gay Science* was published and here we come across the statement 'God is dead' as well as many other passages that are developed in *Thus Spoke Zarathustra*. Its importance rests not only in its literary style, but that it contains the fullest exposition so far of his theories on the will to power, the Superman and the eternal recurrence.

Zarathustra is a prophet, an historical figure who possibly existed around 1500 BC and is also known by the name the Greeks gave him, 'Zoroaster'. Zoroastrianism became the official religion of the mighty Persian Empire for around 1000 years, and small groups still exist in Iran and amongst the Parsis in India. The original Zarathustra invented the concept of good and evil as an eternal war of battling opposites. However, Nietzsche's Zarathustra aimed to show that we must go beyond the concepts of good and evil. For Nietzsche, the historical Zarathustra represents what can be achieved through the will to power, and his belief that every person is responsible for his or her own destiny would have rung a chord with Nietzsche.

Thus Spoke Zarathustra is in four parts, the first part being penned in 1883 and the fourth part completed in 1885. When Nietzsche started writing this work he had recently lost his 'family' of Lou Salomé and Paul Rée, and he now, more than ever, felt alone in the world. *Zarathustra* is about solitude and the hero of the book is the loneliest of men. Zarathustra the prophet has returned with a new teaching, having realized the 'error' of his old prophecy. The book is written in a biblical style, with a narrative, characters, events, setting and plot. In these respects it is very different from all of Nietzsche's other works and helps to explain its appeal to a more popular audience.

At first choosing solitude in the mountains, Zarathustra grows weary of his own company and descends to seek companions and to teach his new philosophy. But, even when surrounded by disciples, he retreats once more back into his solitude and praises its virtues. The new teaching that Zarathustra presents is based upon the foundation that 'God is dead' and, subsequent to this, the teachings on and striving to become the Superman, the will to power and the eternal recurrence.

A brief summary of *Thus Spoke Zarathustra*

The Zarathustra of the Persians was the first prophet to talk of the Day of Judgement, of time reaching a final end. However, Nietzsche's Zarathustra provides a very different teaching:

Part I

> *'All gods are dead: now we want the Superman to live'* – let this be our last will one day at the great noontide.
>
> (*TSZ*, Of the Bestowing Virtue)

Zarathustra descends from ten years of solitude in the mountains and expresses the need for a new teaching to replace the old teaching of a belief in God and morality. The new teaching, 'God is dead', will be brought by another teacher, not Zarathustra, but a 'Superman'. However, the masses laugh at Zarathustra and so he sets out to find followers. In this first part it is Zarathustra who perhaps learns more rather than actually teaches as he realizes that concepts such as the Superman cannot easily be taught. It is not enough to simply tell the people about the Superman through a series of statements. By the end of Part I he has instead gathered together a small band of disciples rather than attempt to preach to the masses. It is a realization on the part of Zarathustra – and Nietzsche too – that his words are not for Everyman.

Part II

> I go new ways, a new speech has come to me; like all creators, I have grown weary of the old tongues. My spirit no longer wants to walk on worn-out soles.
>
> (*TSZ*, The Child and the Mirror)

Having told his disciples to leave him and to find their own way, Zarathustra now looks within himself for enlightenment, returning once more to the mountains. After the passing of years, Zarathustra once again descends amongst his disciples with a 'new speech'. In *Of Self-Overcoming*, he talks of the will to power and states that the highest human beings, those who know how to utilize the will to power in the most positive sense, are philosophers. These philosophers, these Supermen, will destroy the values that people have cherished and replace them with new values. They will teach mankind how to love the earth.

Part III

> 'Behold, we know what you teach: that all things recur eternally and we ourselves with them, and that we have already existed an infinite number of times before and all things with us.'
>
> (*TSZ*, The Convalescent)

This part acts as the climax for the previous two parts. Writing this part, for Nietzsche, was, he reported, the happiest time of his life. For Nietzsche, writing was a form of therapy, but also he believed that reading his works could be therapeutic for the reader. Philosophy as therapy may seem a relatively new idea, but in fact it was something Nietzsche acknowledged too. Zarathustra separates from his disciples and takes a long sea voyage, for he no longer needs disciples. In solitude once more, Zarathustra wills for eternal recurrence, for his 'redemption'.

Part IV

> If you want to rise high, use your own legs! Do not let yourselves be carried up, do not sit on the backs and heads of strangers!
>
> (*TSZ*, Of the Higher Man)

Nietzsche had originally intended Part III to be the final. When he wrote a fourth part he only distributed it to around 20 people. It was added in 1892 when Nietzsche had gone insane and was in no position to object to its conclusion. In this part, Zarathustra's solitude is broken by a series of visitors, including a soothsayer, two kings, a scholar, a sorcerer, the last Pope who also believes that God is dead, the 'ugliest man', the beggar and Zarathustra's own shadow! Zarathustra has a 'last supper' with his visitors proceeded by a speech about the Superman. He then engages in question and answer conversation on such issues as the Superman and the death of God.

Many scholars have argued that *Zarathustra* is a better book without the fourth part. However, although the work is certainly more consistent with only the first three parts, the fourth part is very important in terms of understanding Nietzsche's development as a philosopher. Part IV deals with a major concern of Nietzsche: redemption. In *The Birth of Tragedy*, Nietzsche argued that mankind could be redeemed through the revival of Greek tragedy and the renewal of German culture. However, as he became disillusioned with the possibilities of Art to achieve this, Nietzsche still avoided the pessimistic response and believed that there still can be redemption, that there is still a need to revalue all values and overcome decadence. However, Part IV is less naïve as the ironic realization dawns that affirming life can only be achieved by resenting life as it presently is.

The eternal recurrence

A central theme of *Thus Spoke Zarathustra* is the eternal recurrence. In fact, for Zarathustra, embracing the concept was, for him, salvation. What did Nietzsche mean by this? Apart from *Zarathustra*, the doctrine of the eternal recurrence only gets a few mentions in his later works. However, the doctrine was hinted at in *The Gay Science* where Nietzsche presents a 'what if' image. He asks what if a demon were to creep up to you one night when you are all alone and feeling lonely and were to say to you that the life you have lived and continue to live will be the same life you will live again and again for infinity. This life will be *exactly* the same; no additions and no omissions, every pain, every joy, every small and great event. If this were the case, would you cry out in despair over such a prospect, or would you think it to be the most wonderful outlook ever?

Though not mentioned specifically, this 'what if' scenario sums up the eternal recurrence: whatever in fact happens has happened an infinite number of times in the exact same detail and will continue to do so for eternity. You have lived your life an infinite number of times in the past and will do so an infinite number of times in the future. Importantly, like seemingly the doctrine of the will to power, Nietzsche presents the eternal recurrence as a thought experiment, not a provable truth. You do not have to believe the demon is telling the truth, merely to consider the prospect of it being true and the psychological effect this has upon you. Consider the possibility yourself: does it make you happy or fill you with despair? Like the will to power, the aim is to provide an insight into the way we live our lives and, perhaps, even to change the way we live our lives. If indeed we experience despair at the prospect of living this life again and again then it logically follows that we are not happy with the way we live our lives.

Nietzsche considered that merely thinking of the possibility is the greatest of thoughts and would have an impact on how you perceive yourself and how you live the rest of your life. This is why he gave it such central importance in *Zarathustra*. Proof is not important here, only the fact that we may consider it as even a possibility is sufficient. Nietzsche's aim in presenting the eternal recurrence was to present a positive doctrine of an 'afterlife'; one that would not devalue this life. In this way it is much more powerful than the religious view of heaven. The Christian view of the afterlife, Nietzsche thought, acts as a consolation and causes people to accept their lot in this life with the prospect of a better life when they die.

Nietzsche was not original in presenting the idea of the eternal recurrence. In *Untimely Meditations* he had criticized the doctrine of eternal recurrence that existed in the Ancient Greek philosophy of Pythagoras. Nietzsche's criticism of it at that time was that events do not and cannot recur within the span of known history. If Nietzsche did not accept eternal recurrence as understood by Pythagorean philosophy, then can we speculate over what Nietzsche himself meant by it? Apart from the Ancient Greek philosophers, Nietzsche came across the theory in a more contemporary sense in a writer he much admired, the great German poet Heinrich Heine (1797–1856). In one of his works, Heine refers to time being infinite whereas the things in time, concrete bodies, are finite. He then speculates that if this is the case, given an infinite amount of time, the atoms that have dispersed will eventually reform exactly as before. Therefore, we will be born again in the same form. However, the real impetus for the eternal recurrence was Schopenhauer who considered it to be the most terrible idea possible, an image of endless suffering.

Is this some basis for Nietzsche's belief in the eternal recurrence? The reader must be reminded that, as with the will to power, Nietzsche was not primarily setting out to prove his doctrine, yet, also like the will to power, it is important to consider the problems with it and what foundational basis, if any, there can be for such a doctrine. Although Nietzsche did not present a proof in his published writings, he wrote a great deal in his notes. However, in making use of Nietzsche's notes, we need to be very careful and not equate the idle and often careless scribbling with what Nietzsche was prepared to present as the final work. It is largely because Nietzsche's sister, Elisabeth, proceeded to publish his notes after he went insane that people accepted them as his own philosophy which led to a misunderstanding of the philosopher.

Bearing this cautionary note in mind, Nietzsche's own speculations on the doctrine can be presented as a useful intellectual exercise. Taken from his notes, we can summarize an attempt at a proof as a series of premises with a conclusion:

1. The sum total of energy in the universe is infinite.
2. The number of states of energy is finite.
3. Energy is conserved.
4. Time is infinite.
5. Energy has infinite duration.

This summary bears a strong resemblance to Heine. We can see what Nietzsche is getting at here, rather like the classic example of a monkey in front of a typewriter who, given an infinite amount of time will eventually write the complete works of Shakespeare. The monkey is typing away in a random manner but, in time, the correct combination of letters will be achieved. Likewise, the states of energy are random but, given an infinite amount of time, will reconstitute themselves.

However, there are a number of problems with this:

- Nietzsche relies upon two basic assumptions: that time is infinite (it has no beginning or end) and that the 'states of energy', the matter of the universe, is finite. These, of course, are assumptions that may not in fact be the case and are yet to be proven one way or the other. Much of modern cosmology argues that the universe began with a 'Big Bang' and does have a limited time-span; however it is anybody's guess what existed before the Big Bang or what will occur once the universe ceases to exist.

- It may well be the case that you would live this life again and again for infinity, but this would not motivate you to live this life to the full because, if such a theory were true, it would also mean that every conceivable combination of events would also occur. You can imagine the *worst* life possible: the most miserable, deprived and painful existence that you could live, and you will live it again and again, *no matter what you do in this life*. Nietzsche can only get around this by accepting a deterministic view that not all *possible* combinations can occur, only a return of those combinations that have *actually occurred* in human history. On this issue, Nietzsche does seem to present both possibilities in his notes.

• Georg Simmel presented an elegant rejection of the view that states must recombine given an infinite amount of time. Imagine three wheels of the same size rotating on the same axis. On the circumference of each wheel a mark is placed so that all three wheels are aligned. The wheels are then rotated, but at different speeds. If the second wheel is rotated at twice the speed of the first and the third wheel was $1/\pi$ of the speed of the first, the original alignment would never recur no matter how much time elapsed. Nietzsche, however, may retort that his 'states of energy' are random, whereas Simmel's wheels maintain a constant speed. If they ran at random speeds then they would eventually re-align.

It is curious that he places greater emphasis on this doctrine in his notes and letters than any other aspect of his philosophy, and yet he never elaborated upon it in his published works. When we consider what was important for Nietzsche, what stands out is his belief throughout his life that existence should be *justified*, that is, the true philosopher does not go through life happily in an unquestioning manner, but seeks to give meaning and value to his existence. In *The Birth of Tragedy*, Nietzsche thought life could be justified, could have value, through art, or rather 'Art' in the Ancient Greek sense. The Greeks lived a life of 'Dionysian joy'. However, Nietzsche later in life felt that Art was not the salvation he had originally hoped and it was in August 1881, while walking amongst the high mountains in Switzerland, that the thought came to him of the eternal recurrence. With this thought came an experience, a psychological impact that caused him to affirm life and to love it.

This feeling of joy, Nietzsche thought, is the formula for the greatness of the human being, and he is making an essential connection with the doctrine of the Superman. The Superman is one who, like Zarathustra, is able to embrace the doctrine of eternal recurrence and find redemption within it. If, before and after every action, you were to ask: 'Do you want this action to occur again and again for all eternity?' and you could answer in the joyful affirmative then you are exercising the will to power in a positive manner. The weak look to the next life for hope, whereas the strong look to this life.

The Superman

In *Thus Spoke Zarathustra*, the prophet descends from his mountain to teach the Superman. The German word is *Übermensch,* which literally translates as 'Overman'. However, 'Superman' – despite the comic-book connotations and the possibility of misleading people into believing in some super-human figure – remains a common translation. Nietzsche did not invent the term, and would have come across it in the great German poet Goethe (1749–1832) and, in his study as a classical philologist, in the works of the Greek writer Lucian (*c.*120–80 AD). However, it was Nietzsche who gave the term a new meaning.

If we consider *The Gay Science*, Nietzsche uses the term '*Übermensch*' to refer to gods and heroes of, especially, the Ancient Greeks. For him, these were symbols of non-conformity, of those who did not fit within the norm but were prepared to challenge contemporary values and beliefs. This is a theme – the stress on individualism and the realization of one's self – that is evident in Nietzsche's earlier works, and a careful reading of these shows the development of his thought previous to the first appearance of the Nietzschean Superman in *Thus Spoke Zarathustra*.

In his *Second Meditation*, for example, Nietzsche talks about the goal of humanity and that this must rest with its highest specimens. That is, Nietzsche is aware of what mankind is capable of achieving and raises the question of why we usually fail to live up to our potential. There are examples in history of great people, of philosophers, artists and saints, but even they remain 'human, all too human'.

Nietzsche often sings the praises of Napoleon. Not because of his military prowess but because he represents what Nietzsche calls the 'good European'; the person who is not obsessed with the kind of nationalism that was plaguing Germany at the time of Nietzsche. In this arena, Nietzsche also places such figures as Goethe, Beethoven, Caesar and Michelangelo. However, none of these is a 'Superman', but represent certain features that make up the will to power, such as self-mastery, individualism and charisma. Nonetheless, in the end all of these figures still remain 'human, all too human', for Nietzsche is quick to recognize their faults. There has never been a Superman, although Nietzsche sees the ideal as a Caesar but with the soul of Christ. Even Zarathustra is only the herald of the Superman, not one himself.

Importantly, the link with the eternal recurrence is that the Superman is one who will embrace the doctrine: who *can* look to his own life and wish to relive it again and again for infinity. It is an unconditional acceptance of existence, a saying 'Yes' to everything. For Nietzsche, the Superman is an affirmation of life not, like Schopenhauer, a denial of it and a desire for the self to be extinguished.

However, it is one thing to talk of a Superman, of the highest specimen, of greatness, but what would this 'greatness' really mean in terms of our values? Much of Nietzsche's writings have been taken out of context, and none more so than his references to the Superman and a super race. This was not helped by Nietzsche's sister Elisabeth who assured Hitler that it was *he* that her brother had in mind when he talked of the Superman. Yet, by the Superman, Nietzsche did not mean some blond giant dominating and persecuting lesser mortals. Nietzsche talked of a new direction, but a new direction toward *what*? What are the political, moral and practical applications?

An understanding of the will to power and eternal recurrence gives us some indication, but to understand what Nietzsche meant by the Superman we need to consider his later work.

After Zarathustra

From Nietzsche's notes and letters it is evident that the workings of *Thus Spoke Zarathustra* had been preoccupying him for some time, and after the completion of *Zarathustra*, Nietzsche felt exuberated. Although rarely mentioned by name in his works, the hypothesis of the will to power was always there in the background. This theme was developed to some extent in the works to come, which proved to be his finest: *Beyond Good and Evil* (1886), *Towards a Genealogy of Morals* (1887) and *Twilight of the Idols* (written 1888, published 1889). It was a prolific and original period in Nietzsche's life as he gradually abandoned the aphoristic style in favour of a more coherent form.

It was also during this period that Nietzsche was as 'settled' as he would ever be. He had established a routine of spending the summer in Sils-Maria and the winter in Nice. He had got over the Rée-Salomé affair and he had reduced his contact with the outside world to a bare minimum, concentrating on his writing. His health continued to worsen, however, to the extent that he was nearly blind. The fact that he continued to write so prolifically is a credit to his own will to power.

Nietzsche insisted that everything he wrote after *Thus Spoke Zarathustra* was a commentary upon it. However, the Superman is not mentioned again, the eternal recurrence only occasionally mentioned, and the will to power remains, mostly, below the surface. Perhaps to say that his post-*Zarathustra* works are 'commentaries', therefore, is a little exaggerated. They are works of philosophy in their own right and introduce many new ideas and concepts. At the same time, they do help to explain and elaborate upon the concepts previously introduced, especially his next book *Beyond Good and Evil*.

Nihilism

One of the stated aims of *Beyond Good and Evil* was to liberate Nietzsche's Europe from what he considered to be a decline into decadence, nationalism and stupidity. His concerns for the future of Europe turned out to be prophetic, of course, and this helps to understand why Nietzsche himself was often taken to be something of a prophet after his death; an image his sister Elisabeth was more than happy to promote. The title *Beyond Good and Evil* can be misleading, as it suggests that we must cast aside all values, that there are no values and, consequently, the coming of the Superman heralds a breed that can do as it pleases, without any regard or concern for others. This, however, is not what Nietzsche meant to express.

Nietzsche's philosophy, in a desire to give it some kind of label, has sometimes been described as **nihilism**. Coming from the Latin *nihil*, meaning 'nothing', the term suggests negativity and emptiness, of a rejection of all values and a belief in nothing. Yet Nietzsche could be a very positive, joyful and affirmative philosopher. We can categorize two types of nihilism; neither of which Nietzsche falls into but was nonetheless influenced by:

- Oriental nihilism
- European nihilism.

1 Oriental nihilism

Schopenhauer was heavily influenced by what he understood of Buddhist teachings and, when he talks of extinguishing the self and that the world we live in has no ultimate reality, it is this form of nihilism that he is considering. It possesses the following characteristics:

- Because the world we live in is not real our attachment to it is an illusion.
- Life is without sense or point, merely an endless cycle of birth and rebirth.
- To find salvation we must escape from this world and extinguish the concept of the self.

2 European nihilism

The Russian author Ivan Turgenev (1818–83) was the first to introduce the nihilist to the novel. In his greatest novel, *Fathers and Sons* (1862), the hero is Bazarov, an idealistic young radical dedicated to universal freedom but destined for tragedy. This novel reflected a nihilism that existed in the latter decades of nineteenth-century Europe:

- Nihilists consisted mostly of the younger generation who rejected the beliefs and values of the older generation.
- Rejecting the beliefs of their elders such as religion, tradition and culture, these nihilists claimed to believe in 'nothing'.
- However, the nihilists replaced traditional beliefs with a belief in science. Instead of seeking salvation in the next life, the nihilists looked to a better understanding of this world as the future hope.

3 The 'nihilism' of Nietzsche

In both Oriental nihilism and European nihilism, there still exists a belief in salvation; that there can be a form of order and values. Nietzsche, however, goes much further than this:

- All beliefs systems, whether it is science, religion, art, or morality, are fictions. They are merely instances of the will to power.
- This world is the only world, even if it is valueless. There is no 'unity', no 'truth'.
- This fact should not lead to pessimism, to a 'will to nothingness'. Rather, we should adopt a Dionysian 'yes' to life.

To say the world is 'valueless' is not to say that it has little worth. Rather, it does not make sense to say one thing has more 'value' than another, because there is no such thing as a scale of values. Nothing has value; there are no facts, no 'better' or 'worse'. This was a rejection of the beliefs of so many philosophies and religions that there is an objective world. These religions and other metaphysical propositions often endorse a **Correspondence Theory of Truth** (see also next chapter). This theory holds that when we use terms like 'God', or 'good' or 'bad' or 'justice' we are making reference to an actual 'God', an actual 'justice' and so on; that is, these terms *correspond* to a reality. For Nietzsche, there is no reality for these terms to correspond to. Nietzsche's views on truth and perspectivism will be considered in the next chapter.

Amor fati

Amor fati: to love your fate! For European nihilism, especially of the Russian variety, a rejection of traditional values had political implications with the call for a revolution. For Nietzsche, his main concern was with the psychological impact of the acceptance that there are no truths. It could well lead to pessimism and despair or the attitude that 'anything goes'. For Nietzsche, he saw nihilism as a positive affirmation of life, to be freed of the burden of hope in an afterlife, in salvation. You should love your fate without the need of fictions and false securities to comfort you.

Nietzsche's 'nihilism' finds its culmination in the doctrine of the eternal recurrence. Man must not only accept his fate and, indeed love his fate, but also to embrace this purposeless existence as recurring again and again for infinity. The person who can do this deserves the title 'Superman':

- The Superman rejects the belief that there are objective values or values of any kind.
- The Superman does not, as a result, become a pessimist or suffer from despair; rather he embraces life and loves his fate (*amor fati*).
- Even when faced with the prospect that he will have to live exactly the same life again, the Superman's *amor fati* is not dented. Even existence in its most fearful form is a joyful one.

The need for consolation

Nietzsche has presented us with a picture of humanity and its relation to the world it lives in. This picture is of a people constantly trying to impose an order, structure and meaning upon a universe that has no order, structure or meaning. Rather, the universe is in a state of constant change, plurality, chaos and becoming. There is no benign God, no objective moral values, no, in Kantian terms, 'noumena'.

Nietzsche asks why, for probably the whole history of humanity, we cling on to beliefs in God or objective values. There is an obvious need for religious and metaphysical comfort. However, as Nietzsche's world approached the twentieth century, there was a growing feeling that such beliefs no longer had intellectual credibility. A belief in God was filled with too many paradoxes and contradictions, too many claims to truth that conflicted with the evidence.

As more and more people began to question religious claims they looked for other 'truths' through science, through art, or through Kantian metaphysics. Yet, for Nietzsche, this was just replacing one fiction with another. Having said that, during his earlier writings, notably in *The Birth of Tragedy*, Nietzsche attributed value to art. Nietzsche recognized that art can help to give meaning to life and to gain access to a different way of understanding the world. Although Nietzsche recognized the psychological benefits of art, it was another thing to believe that art is any 'truer' than any other belief. This is not something that Nietzsche would subscribe to.

Nietzsche always took an interest in science, too. He recognized that science provided humanity with many benefits. Whereas religion was concerned with the next life, with salvation and the eternal soul, science at least provided knowledge of the world that might endure the scepticism of generations. Here, however, we can see some contradictions in Nietzsche's own thinking for, at times, he places a great emphasis upon science that seems to go against his own view that there are no 'facts'. But, although impressed with the methods of scientific investigation, later in life he adopted the view that science, too, rested on errors. Science, like art, is creation and invention rather than discovery, for there is nothing there to 'discover'. Undoubtedly science is *useful*, but this is different from believing that science is *true*. This realization, that all beliefs are simply a matter of perspective, is the first step that must be made if man is to *overcome* man.

Summary

- *Thus Spoke Zarathustra* is Nietzsche's most popular work. It develops the themes of the will to power, the Superman and the eternal recurrence.

- The principal idea of the eternal recurrence is that whatever in fact happens has happened an infinite number of times in the exact same detail and will do so for eternity.

- Nietzsche did not set out to prove the doctrine of the eternal recurrence; rather to present it as a thought experiment and to challenge us to consider what our reaction would be *if* the doctrine were true.

- The Superman is someone who is prepared to embrace the doctrine of eternal recurrence and to look forward to the possibility of living his/her life over and over forever.

- Although the term 'Superman' is the usual translation of the German *Übermensch,* this does not imply a super-human being. Rather it requires humanity to adopt a certain psychological stance towards the world and to consider the possibility of adopting new values.

- Nietzsche's nihilism was not a belief in 'nothing' and the resulting view that 'anything goes'. Rather, it is a rejection that there are objective values of any kind.

- Nietzsche adopted the stance of *amor fati*; that you should love your own fate and embrace the doctrine of eternal recurrence.

07

on truth and perspectivism

In this chapter you will learn:

- what Nietzsche means by 'truth'
- about his use of the term 'perspectivism'
- about the value placed on reason and on language.

Assuming that truth is a woman – what then? Is there not reason to suspect that all philosophers, in so far as they were dogmatists, have known very little about women?

(*BGE*, Preface)

One important field of philosophy is known as **epistemology,** or the theory of knowledge. In fact a number of philosophers would argue that this field is *the* most important task for philosophers to undergo: what can we know with any certainty? The word 'philosopher' is from the Greek 'lover of wisdom' and whilst the term 'wisdom' seems to be rarely used these days to describe knowledge, the primary task of philosophers is the same and goes right back to the Greeks who asked the questions that still engage us today. How 'wise' can we be? That is, how much can we know and what do we mean when we say we 'know' something to be the case?

For example, someone may feel inclined to make a seemingly innocent remark such as 'the sky is very blue today'. The philosophical response to this would be to raise questions concerning the validity of the statement 'the sky is very blue today'. For example, is the sky very blue for everybody? When we say it is blue what colour are we perceiving in our heads? Is the sky itself actually blue or do we only see it as blue? What is meant by *very* blue as opposed to just blue? How blue can blue be? Would the sky be blue if there was no one around to see it? Can we really know for sure what colour the sky actually is? And so on! In fact, the last question gets to the heart of epistemology. We are unable to step outside of our own bodies. We cannot 'see' the world as it actually is because we see it via our senses. Can we always trust our senses?

Varieties of truth

It might seem odd to talk about 'varieties' of truth, for surely there is just truth. But philosophers have presented a number of different understandings of truth. There is absolute truth (something is true absolutely under any circumstances); contingent truth (the truth is dependent upon place, time and so on); necessary truth (given a set of statements, something has to be true and cannot be otherwise); scientific truth; mathematical truth; relative truth, and so on. However, most philosophical understanding of truth can be divided into two: the correspondence theory of truth and the coherence theory of truth.

The correspondence theory of truth

This is the most common notion of truth. This asks whether a proposition actually corresponds to something in the 'real world'. For example, if someone says 'that car is red' while pointing to a red car, then that statement corresponds to a reality. If, at the time, they are actually pointing to a brown dog then it can be shown that the statement does not correspond. Effectively the correspondence theory states that there is a relation between statements of belief ('that car is red') and the actual state of affairs (there is an actual red car there). Its attraction is in its intuitive appeal, but Nietzsche sets out to attack this theory especially.

The coherence theory of truth

This evaluates the truth of statements by relating them to other proven truths within a system of thought. It might help to conceive of truth as a web of beliefs: those beliefs at the centre of the web are the most enduring, such as the belief that other people exist, that we all have to die someday, that the sun gives heat and light, and so on. The further we go from the centre of the web, the less solid and permanent are our beliefs. Some beliefs that were more central have now drifted to the edges. However, so long as they fit together, the web remains intact. If a belief is so inconsistent with our other beliefs then it is so far on the outskirts of the web so as to be ignored by most, or it is rejected altogether. In this view, there may be no claims to absolute truths, only their coherence.

Nietzsche would not deny that we *want* to have correspondence truth or that we *believe* that statements correspond to actuality. In fact Nietzsche states in *Genealogy of Morals* amongst other works that we *will* truth. If we look for Truth in an objective sense, with a capital 'T', it involves turning our back on this and looking for something 'out there'; something that, for Nietzsche, does not exist in any comprehensible way. It is therefore a pointless exercise and also detrimental for humanity because of its deflection from this life. Whatever knowledge we have is always from a perspective and this fact is unavoidable. Even though the world we experience is shaped by our own perception and perspective, and it has no more substance than a supposed 'other world', it is nonetheless the one we are able to live in. Despite the view of some Nietzsche scholars, Nietzsche himself would not have considered himself a subscriber to coherent truth and nor does he subscribe to pragmatic truth (we should accept knowledge of the world provided it is practical and workable). Rather, Nietzsche presents us with truth perspectivism.

Nietzsche's perspectivism

What then in the last resort are the truths of mankind? They are the irrefutable errors of mankind.

(*GS*, 265)

Imagine you are staring at a painting, and that this painting represents the sum of all life and experience. The painting, you might think, is finished. The paint is dry and it hangs upon the wall. For Nietzsche, however, he is not gazing at a finished painting, for it is still evolving and will continue to do so forever. Most people accept 'common sense': that there is a world out there, that when you kick a stone there is an actual stone, that the laws and behaviour so embedded within our lives are so real that they are not questioned. The painting is thick with paint and it is difficult to wipe aside the colours and shapes of earlier generations. For Nietzsche, however, our 'common sense' is merely an *interpretation*. This is Nietzsche's **perspectivism**: we see the world from our own accumulated lives and experiences, but this does not make it *right*. The painting is not an accurate representation of something 'out there', but the imaginings of the human mind.

Nietzsche's perspectivism raises more questions than it answers because Nietzsche does not really go out of his way to explain in any detail what he means by perspectivism. For example, are there groups of perspectives such as the religious perspective or the scientific perspective, or are there individual perspectives so that each person has a different perspective from another? One important point that Nietzsche makes in, for example, *The Antichrist*, is worth stressing: 'truth and the belief that something is true: two completely diverse worlds of interest' (*AC* 23). In other words, a perspective is *not* the same as a belief or a set of beliefs; so to say 'I believe the sky is very blue today' is not the same as having a perspective. Nietzsche is being much more radical than that, but if it isn't a belief then what is it? Nietzsche, to put it bluntly, does not help us out here!

It may help to go back to one of Nietzsche's earlier works, an essay called 'On Truth and Lie in a Morally-Disengaged Sense', written just a year after *The Birth of Tragedy*, but never published. In this work, Nietzsche looked at Greek culture through 'the perspective of life' rather than any kind of absolute standpoint and here we already have the germ of Nietzsche's perspectivism that it is simply impossible to see things from a 'perspectiveless perspective'. In the essay Nietzsche says that there is a generally accepted way of seeing things. For example, in morality, it is generally considered that lying is bad and telling the truth is good. But from the 'perspective of life' things can look different: weaker people often preserve themselves by lying, cheating, flattering, deceiving and so on. So from that perspective – the perspective of surviving – lying can be seen as a positive thing.

The influence of Kant can be seen here in the sense that Nietzsche acknowledged that human beings can only know things from a human perspective, but Nietzsche went much further than Kant in denying that there is a single human perspective. Rather, there are lots of different human perspectives depending upon time, place, group, physiology, environmental conditions, stronger and weaker types, and so on:

In fact all tables of values – all 'you ought to's' – which we know from history or ethnological research, in any case, first require a physiological examination and interpretive explication, before even a psychological one; similarly, all of them stand in need of a critique from the side of medical science.

(*GM*, Essay 1, Section 17)

Common sense, the acceptance that things are how we think they are, is not only seen as necessary for life, but also useful. Nietzsche would not disagree with this. Our 'painting' of the world is not a random collection of colours and shapes, but a purposeful process of understanding the world and adapting to it; that is, our worldview is necessary for our very survival. To this extent, 'common sense' is 'true' in that it allows us to function. This understanding of 'truth' is equated with *utility*: how *useful* is interpretation of the world? By declaring that God is dead, Nietzsche is stating that the belief in God no longer serves a useful purpose. Nietzsche's nihilism, then, is not a rejection of common sense; it is not the discarding of a painting that has taken generations to construct. To do so would not only be foolhardy, but impractical. Rather, Nietzsche's nihilism is a rejection that common sense is really 'true' in any objective sense; that is perfect, immutable and complete. 'Truth', therefore, is an evolving process. This may suggest a pragmatic theory of truth in his rejection of the belief in God and it is understandable that a number of scholars have suggested this, but Nietzsche remains ambiguous. Whilst he generally accepts that what is 'true' has been throughout history equated with what is stable, reliable and workable, this is not to say that Nietzsche himself therefore accepts them as 'true' in a pragmatic sense, especially as his interest in 'health' requires himself at least to be 'un-pragmatic' and prefer falsehoods. At the same time, it could be argued that Nietzsche is being pragmatic here in his advocating health as life-enhancing.

Also, at times, Nietzsche can be quite dismissive of 'illusions' because they do not represent what is really true. In *Human, All Too Human*, Nietzsche speculated that there might indeed be a metaphysical world, but at the very best this is just a bare possibility and much too inadequate to look to it for salvation. Here, however, there seems an inconsistency in Nietzsche's thought: is there a 'real' world or isn't there? Truth, for Nietzsche, seems to be equated with 'workable fictions' yet he also seems to want to say what the world is actually *like*. Here he becomes muddled; on the one hand declaring that the world is a matter of perspective, whilst on the other not entirely denying the possibility that we can have endurable facts. As an example, it is a 'fact' that humans need oxygen to breathe. Are we to say that this is a matter merely of perspective, a 'truth' that we need to survive but that we cannot say that *there really is oxygen, and we really need it*? Are we then presented with a hierarchy of knowledge, some more 'true' than others? Even if Nietzsche were to say, as he seems to, that our understanding of the world all boils down to aspects of the will to power, there is a danger here of introducing his own metaphysics: a 'force' that prevails across the universe.

Reason and the senses

Nietzsche not only was frequently given the title of a nihilist, but also an irrationalist. Nietzsche, however, was not against reason. What Nietzsche was against was anything that is not *useful*, anything that makes life impossible. His criticism was not against reason, but against rationalist philosophers such as Plato. Plato emphasized reason at the expense of the senses and this world. His rationalism took him into another realm, a belief in rational truth. As a result, Plato considered this world an illusion and a distraction from rational meditation. The senses can give us grounds for belief, but never true knowledge. Nietzsche held that reason couldn't be accepted at the expense or neglect of the senses. Even in his later work, *The Twilight of the Idols* (1889), Nietzsche continues to hold that the senses allow us to sharpen our beliefs and teach us to think. Nietzsche here is not being 'irrational' in an emotive, animal sense. Although he also believed that the passions are important and that they can teach us, he saw the role of the senses as an educative tool that enables us to observe the world and fine-tune our perspective of it.

The importance of language

If we consider the history of thought we become aware that this history is almost entirely full of a belief in gods, a God, an afterlife, and the eternal soul. It is only very recently, representing a small fraction of this timeline, that people have begun to question these concepts. Now, returning to our painting once more: if every brush stroke represents 100 years of the history of mankind, then the questioning of metaphysical concepts amounts to only one such brushstroke, hidden amongst thousands of others. If our worldview is painted in such a way, Nietzsche asserted that so, also, is our language. In *Twighlight of the Idols*, Nietzsche famously declared that we would not get rid of God until we get rid of grammar. This view was echoed later by the British philosopher Bertrand Russell (1872–1970) who believed that everyday language embodies the metaphysics of the Stone Age. If we are to establish a better philosophy then we must work out a new language.

Nietzsche argues that the language they speak seduces men. When people use terms such as 'mind' or 'soul' it is so embedded within our language that, as Nietzsche says, we would rather break a bone in our body than break a word. Most of our language is based upon mankind's early use of language, upon a more primitive psychology that we therefore cannot escape from because of our use of everyday language. When we use a word we still remain attached to the commonsense view that the word actually *refers* to something, rather than it being the product of mankind many generations ago:

> What, then, is truth? A manoeuvrable army of metaphors, metonymies, anthropomorphisms – in short, a summation of human relationships which have been poetically and rhetorically heightened, transposed, and embellished, and which, after long use by a people, are

considered to be solid, canonical, and binding: truths are illusions whose true nature has been forgotten.

(On Truth and Lie in a Morally-Disengaged Sense)

Our attachment to our language is so strong we could not readily do without the fictions it describes. Nietzsche also believed that even the language of physics is a fiction, an interpretation to suit us. He talks of the concept of atoms as a useful tool to explain the nature of the universe, but that is all that they are. However, Nietzsche's perspectivism goes much further than this for it is not just theoretical entities such as atoms, but *all entities* that are fictions. All bodies, lines, surfaces, concepts of cause and effect and of motion; these are all just articles of faith but do not in themselves constitute a proof.

Nietzsche asks why it is necessary to believe in such concepts as cause and effect. He does not entirely accept the Kantian view that we have 'human spectacles' and that we therefore have no choice but to perceive the world in a certain way. Rather we have learnt through harsh experience that the way we perceive the world is the most suitable for survival. There may well have been many people who have seen the world in a different way but, as a consequence, have perished. The view of causality that Nietzsche presents is not very different from David Hume's. Hume argued that we arrive at the concept of cause and effect not because causality actually exists in nature, but because, through habit, we conjoin one event with another. Therefore, causality is a product of the mind, but a necessary product nonetheless. For Nietzsche they are conventional fictions that are useful for communication.

There have been philosophers and scientists who have also rejected the world of 'common sense', but Nietzsche asserts that they then make the mistake of creating another world that they consider to be real. Despite Nietzsche's charity towards science, he does not accept that it has brought us any closer to reality because, for Nietzsche, there is no 'reality'. Since the time of Galileo in the seventeenth century it has been the practice of scientists to present theories that conflict with the contemporary commonsense view of the world, such as the view that the earth revolves around the sun or that humanity evolved from other species. This has resulted in often radical transformations in our understanding of the world and leads to a new commonsense view. For the scientist, these theories are usually regarded as allowing us to get closer to how the universe really is. For Nietzsche, despite their pragmatic application, they are still nonetheless a fiction. They are no more 'real' than the previous worldview.

Nietzsche could never persuade himself to adopt an absolute idealist stance that there is no world outside the mind. This is because he believed, like Kant, that there is a world out there, but a world so different, so unwilling to be tied to our desire for an ordered and structured universe, that it is impossible to even so much as conceive of this world, let alone talk about it. Nietzsche, therefore, does not entirely escape from Kant's clutches and, as he grew older, Nietzsche speculated more about this 'real' world. Inevitably, however, as soon as one attempts to talk about the 'real' world we are immediately tongue-tied by the limitations of our language. Because we have no other language we are sucked into using metaphysical terms that tie us to our worldview. Although we may not have any other language, we can perhaps 'play' with language. Certainly, Nietzsche's aphoristic style, his clever play on words and his confrontational and controversial idioms, force us to question and think. Not unlike mystical traditions that employ poetry, riddle, 'koans' and so on in an attempt to describe the indescribable, Nietzsche is also compelled to use similar methods. This may well give his philosophy a 'mystical' quality, but perhaps this is unavoidable.

Does Nietzsche's perspectivism help to provide us with a clearer understanding of the Superman? Nietzsche's *Übermensch* would not be deluded into believing in a reality that can be attained or comprehended, nor would he look to religion or philosophy for salvation. He would be less concerned with stating what is true than in telling what is false, yet he would also need to be tied to a commonsense perspective if he were to survive; the extreme sceptic would not be able to get out of bed in the mornings. However, this should not prevent daring experimentation, in seeking a new language and philosophy. Would Nietzsche go so far as to suggest a *physical* change also? Is he pre-empting the advances in genetic engineering? This, one suspects, would be giving the German philosopher too much credit.

Summary

• Nietzsche believed that there is no 'true' way of seeing the world. It is all a matter of perspective. However, what matters is whether our view of the world is useful or not.

• Nietzsche did not reject reason at the expense of the senses or the 'passions'.

• He recognized the importance of language in structuring the way we perceive the world.

• He was not an idealist for he believed there is a real world out there, but we are unable to say anything about it and it is a waste of time to even speculate upon it.

08

Nietzsche and religion

In this chapter you will learn:

- about Nietzsche's 'religiosity'
- the effect his Lutheran upbringing had on his philosophy
- about Nietzsche's 'religious experience'
- why Nietzsche valued religion
- about the importance of myth
- about the role of religion in the State
- about Nietzsche and Islam
- about Nietzsche and Buddhism.

I have a terrible fear I shall one day be pronounced holy
... I do not want to be a saint, rather even a buffoon.

(*EH*, Why I Am Destiny 1)

Nietzsche's religiosity

Nietzsche has often been described in the past as an atheist, and his declaration 'God is dead' would seem to support such a view. Yet an essential appeal of his philosophy is his use of religious language, metaphors and symbols; together with the fact that Nietzsche himself does not escape entirely from his Lutheran upbringing. Further, Nietzsche was specifically addressing an audience at a specific time and place (that is the coming new century in Europe) and what Nietzsche perceived to be an important turning-point for Europe: the dawn of a new age in which the old God was dead and society was confronted with an increase in the secularization process. But Nietzsche's 'religiosity' rests in his lack of 'faith' in the secular order to provide humanity with any meaningful existence.

Some scholars of the past have certainly acknowledged that Nietzsche has a 'religiosity'. For example, the philosopher Martin Heidegger called him, 'that passionate seeker after God and the last German philosopher' and, more recently, Erich Heller says of him that, 'He is, by the very texture of his soul and mind, one of the most radically religious natures that the nineteenth century brought forth ...'

More modern writers such as Alistair Kee in *Nietzsche Against the Crucified* and Giles Fraser in *Redeeming Nietzsche* have argued that Nietzsche is very much a religious philosopher, summed up in the following quotes:

> Nietzsche came to describe himself as an atheist, but we should not try to understand him within that long tradition of philosophers who have joined battle with theologians over the traditional proofs for the existence of God ... his position is so much more profound and complex that to describe him as an atheist, while not false, is liable to mislead.

(Kee, *Nietzsche Against the Crucified*, p.27)

I will want to argue that Nietzsche's atheism is not *premised*, either intellectually or emotionally, upon a denial of the existence of God. This is not to say I believe Nietzsche did after all believe in God. Clearly he didn't. Nietzsche was unquestionably an atheist – my question is going to be: of what sort?

(Fraser, *Redeeming Nietzsche*, p.22)

Nietzsche as a 'sort' of atheist

Nietzsche, then, may not be an atheist in a traditional sense, but in a particular sense: an atheist in the sense of not believing in God, but at the same time not lacking in some form of religiosity. At the very least, Nietzsche did declare himself a devotee of the Greek god Dionysus. Nietzsche's Lutheran upbringing cannot be totally discarded, for although Nietzsche may not be concerned with the existence or otherwise of God – and does not bother to engage in any of the standard arguments for or against the existence of God – he nonetheless deals with, in the words of the theologian Paul Tillich, what is of 'ultimate concern': how are we to be 'saved'? By 'saved' this need not require the baggage of theological teachings related to salvation, for it is enough to conceive salvation as a concern for the future of the human race *on this earth*. Nietzsche's concern is to replace what he perceived as a pathologically sick belief in a Christian God with a new life-affirming framework for salvation.

An important reason why Nietzsche uses Christian imagery and ideas even though 'God is dead' is that the death of God does not bring theology to an end, rather to a fresh beginning: the death of God is what makes salvation possible. In *Twilight of the Idols*, Nietzsche remarks, 'We deny God; in denying God we deny accountability: only by doing *that* do we redeem the world.' To do this Nietzsche reaches for Christian imagery.

Nietzsche the Lutheran

It was only out of the soil of the German Reformation
that there could grow a Nietzsche.

(Dietrich Bonhoeffer)

A number of factors contribute to Nietzsche's religious outlook:
the tight-knit Lutheran background, the influence of his father –
a pastor – his piety as a child, the key places of his upbringing
all being at the geographical centre of Lutheranism, and
enrolment to study theology at the University of Bonn. In fact,
Nietzsche saw Luther as one of his heroes up until the time he
split with Wagner, and Nietzsche is deeply indebted to Lutheran
Pietism, the movement that was prevalent in the time and place
of Nietzsche's upbringing. Pietism is essentially anti-rationalist,
indifferent to theological speculation and concerned more with
'instinct', with engaging with Christ on a personal rather than
an intellectual level. This emphasis upon instinct is central to
Nietzsche's philosophy, as this quote from *The Antichrist*
highlights:

> It is false to the point of absurdity to see in a 'belief'... the
> distinguishing characteristic of the Christian: only
> Christian *practice*, a life such as he who died on the Cross
> *lived*, is Christian ... Even today *such* a life is possible, for
> *certain* men even necessary: genuine primitive
> Christianity will be possible at all times ... *Not* a belief
> but a doing ...
>
> (*AC*, 33)

Whilst, as already stated (see Chapter 07), Nietzsche is not
against rationalism as such, he considered it more important to
trust your instincts, to be led by your passions, as he writes to
his friend Peter Gast: 'I have a taste, but it rests upon no
reasons, no logic, and no imperative.' In the case of religion, it
is our 'taste' that decides whether we engage with it or not,
rather than reason. Nietzsche's pietism has been associated with
his *amor fati* (see Chapter 06): to hate life is blasphemous.
Whilst Nietzsche has been called a nihilist, Nietzsche himself

sees Christianity as nihilistic, as life-denying and depraved, in which life can only have meaning by reference to some other-worldly realm. With the death of God, this nihilism is unmasked and Europe is faced with apparent hopelessness, devoid of salvation. At this point, the point at which Nietzsche believed existed in Europe during his time, the post-moral period, Nietzsche sees the opportunity to address the question of whether humanity really needs redemption from the divine: cannot human life be self-affirming? Throughout Nietzsche's philosophy is a sense of urgency, a recognition that there existed in his time a very brief window of opportunity, for the power of *ressentiment*, of self-hatred, a potent use of the will to power, and would quickly regroup under another guise with new prophets. One reason why Nietzsche is so widely read today must be due to the recognition that these new salvations have come under such brands as communism, nationalism, capitalism and so on.

Salvation, for Nietzsche, is an *internal* transcendence. It is a healing process to cure humanity of what he saw as a disease brought about by attempts to ameliorate suffering through Christian redemption. However, rather than healing, Christianity has made the patient worse. Nietzsche's conception of health is not that of a pain-free state, for he believed pain to be a prerequisite of health. Nietzsche believed that Christianity does not cure, it *anaesthetizes*: it blocks pain and persuades the people that the absence of pain is the same as salvation.

Nietzsche and 'inspiration'

Mention has already been made of Nietzsche's curious 'religious' experience beside the lake of Silvaplana (see Chapter 02). In *Ecce Homo*, Nietzsche again refers to this experience: 'It was on these two walks that the whole of the first *Zarathustra* came to me, above all Zarathustra himself, as a type: more accurately, *he stole up on me* ...' (*EH*) and in the same book, Nietzsche says the following:

If one had the slightest residue of superstition left in one, one would hardly be able to set aside the idea that one is merely incarnation, merely mouthpiece, merely medium of overwhelming forces. The concept of revelation, in the sense that something suddenly, with unspeakable certainty and subtlety, becomes visible, audible, simply describes the fact. One hears, one does not seek; one takes, one does not ask who gives; a thought flashes up like lightning, with necessity, unfalteringly formed – I have never had any choice. An ecstasy whose tremendous tension sometimes discharges itself in a flood of tears, while one's steps now involuntarily rush along, now involuntarily lag; a complete being outside oneself with the distinct consciousness of a multitude of subtle shudders and trickling down to one's toes … Everything is in the highest degree involuntary but takes place as in a tempest of a feeling of freedom, of absoluteness, of power, of divinity.

(*EH*)

Such remarks do not suggest a man who lacks a religious outlook. This 'inspiration' is not conceived of in terms of ideas that Nietzsche himself invented, but rather it comes across as a mystical feeling 'of power, of divinity'.

Religion as life-enhancing

For Nietzsche, it is not important whether religion is 'true' or not, but whether or not it is life-enhancing. Perhaps the best way to understand Nietzsche is not as a *global* philosopher full of grand schemes, but a *local* philosopher. When reading Nietzsche it is better to think locally; to find out what his specific target is. For example, Nietzsche does not reject compassion wholesale, but rather compassion which leads to nihilistic ends. He does not attack compassion, self-sacrifice as such – in fact Nietzsche was himself considered a compassionate person by those who knew him – but how it is expressed through such individuals as

Schopenhauer and Paul Rée. It is interesting that both Schopenhauer and Rée, like Nietzsche in certain respects, were atheists, determinists and naturalists, yet Nietzsche goes out of his way to condemn them.

Does he reject the supernatural, the non-empirical? No. Rather he is concerned with what is being *aimed* at here. For example, the belief in Greek gods is quite acceptable because it signified an affirmation of life. Therefore, certain kinds of religion, of the supernatural are equally acceptable. A future society could indeed be supernatural and non-empirical. When Nietzsche writes about religion, when he is either being critical of Christianity or positive about Christ, Buddhism or Islam, his ultimate value is health: what promotes greater health? What he means by this, in a seemingly Freudian sense (and perhaps even Platonic), is that our selves – our 'soul' if you will – is fragmented. Humans are, for the most part, fragmented with drives all over the place.

On Islam

Interestingly, Nietzsche makes over 100 references to Islam and Islamic cultures in his works. At times he pours great praise on Islam and admires the people and virtues of the Muslim poet Hafiz. He talks of the great achievements of Muslim Spain and sees Islam as a life-affirming religion in opposition to the life-denying Christianity of his time. At the same time, Nietzsche can come across as incredibly ignorant and **Orientalist** (this is a term used to describe western writings and writers who present a romantic and distorted picture of the east, or the 'Orient') in his perception of Islam and the Islamic world which was by no means an uncommon perception for Europeans at this time: Islam seen as a manipulative instrument of social engineering, the Prophet Muhammad as a cunning impostor, and so on. In fact Nietzsche read quite a lot of Orientalist texts, including William Palgrave, Julius Wellhausen and Max Muller.

Leaving aside the contradictory nature of these remarks, the fact that Nietzsche feels so ready to make any remarks at all concerning Islam and its culture is interesting in itself. One scholar, Ian Almond, states that Nietzsche's sympathy and interest in Islam may well be a result of his distaste for German culture. That is to say, Nietzsche exaggerates the features of an 'Other' culture in order to demean his own. This cultural claustrophobia, leading to a romantic longing for the Orient, is not new, especially amongst Romantic poets (in Nietzsche's terms, Heinrich Heine and Goethe especially). Nietzsche never actually visited a Muslim country and his access to sources on Islam would have been, on the whole, Orientalist in their perspective.

In a sense, Nietzsche's Orientalism and the question of how 'correctly' this represents Islam is irrelevant for Nietzsche. What matters is how useful is it. This comes back to Nietzsche's *perspectivism* considered in Chapter 07. What this suggests is that Nietzsche was not so much interested in Islam and Islamic culture as such and, for that matter, was not that learned in it either, but rather he used it as a battering ram against his own culture and, in addition, Islam served an epistemological function by highlighting the weaknesses of European culture and so presenting possible alternatives. Importantly, the appeal of Islam for Nietzsche was that he perceived it as less modern, less democratic, less enlightened and hence, *much better* given his criticism of so-called Enlightened, democratic Europe. As Nietzsche himself said, 'I want to live among Muslims for a good long time, especially where their faith is most devout: in this way I expect to hone my appraisement and my eye for all that is European.'

An example of Nietzsche's perspective on Islam is his admiration for the Assassins: this group, the *Hasishin*, were an outcrop of the Ismaili Shi'a sect and existed from around the eleventh to the thirteenth century. Their primary task seemed to be to engage in being the mediaeval equivalent of suicide bombers, particularly assassinating rulers who they considered to be corrupt and oppressors. Nietzsche was not condoning political assassination here, rather it is Nietzsche's fascination with the Other, and the more seemingly 'Other' the better; his fascination lies with extremities of difference which is reflected in one letter to his sister Elisabeth when he states he wishes to live in Japan.

To illustrate, this is the quote from Section 60 of *The Antichrist*:

> Christianity robbed us of the harvest of the culture of the ancient world, it later went on to rob us of the harvest of the culture of Islam. The wonderful Moorish cultural world of Spain, more closely related to us at bottom, speaking more directly to our senses and taste, than Greece and Rome, was trampled down (I do not say by what kind of feet): why? because it was noble, because it owed its origin to manly instincts, because it said Yes to life even in the rare and exquisite treasures of Moorish life! ... Later on, the Crusaders fought against something they would have done better to lie down in the dust before – a culture compared with which even our nineteenth century may well think itself very impoverished and very 'late' ...

(AC, 60)

Here Nietzsche declares Muslims to be 'one of us', and his regard for Islamic culture as closer than Greece and Rome is quite remarkable considering Nietzsche's own Hellenic leanings.

Myth, modernity and monumental history

If we are looking for recurrent themes in Nietzsche, then undoubtedly a key theme is his criticism of **modernity**, of the way we are now. This theme has occurred in Nietzsche's writings right from his first major work, *The Birth of Tragedy*. The term 'modernity' is a much-bandied one, and is considered to be the result of two important revolutions: the French Revolution and the Industrial Revolution. Henry Cox refers to the 'five pillars' of modernity:

1. the emergence of sovereign national states
2. hegemony of science-based technology
3. bureaucratic rationalism
4. profit maximization as a prime motivator
5. secularization.

In monumental history we have, and we *need*, role models that inspire us to greatness through imitation. For monumental figures to be monumental they must be mythologized, not deconstructed and individualized. Our heroes need to be lacking specific detail, to be blurred around the edges, so that we can fill the gaps with our 'poetic invention'. That is, they have to be flexible in order to be relevant to our modern times. A healthy, thriving culture, for Nietzsche, is one which possesses the 'plastic power' to 'incorporate ... what is past and foreign', to 'recreate the moulds' of the past in the language of the present (*UM* II 1). In a sense, the mythologized figures act as our unwritten laws for a community. Only monumental history is creative, although that is not to say that you should not also be critical. To flourish, Nietzsche says, 'man must possess and from time to time employ the strength to break up and dissolve a part of the past.' How we are to judge this is on the basis of what is life-fulfilling, what makes us grow. Nietzsche is critical of the Christianity of his time because it *poisons* life; this is in contrast to his praise of Jesus as a monumental, mythical figure.

Nietzsche argued that history as it now serves in the world of modernity *atomizes*. Historical events are merely historical facts, a vast 'encyclopaedia' or, in more modern terms, a Wikipedia. Modernity lacks culture, it is a 'fairground motley', a 'chaotic jumble' of confused and different styles (*UM* I 1). In Nietzsche's *Thus Spoke Zarathustra*, Zarathustra both loves and scorns the town known as 'Motley Cow' because its citizens are cow- (herd-) like and yet live in a chaotic jumble of different lifestyles.

This is reminiscent of Plato's criticism of democracy; lots of bright colours but nothing solid. Culture, therefore, represents a unity of the people, a *Volk*. Nietzsche argues that presenting us with a smorgasbord of lifestyle options that have no evaluative ranking produces a mood of confusion and cynicism. Rather than taking *part* in life we become *spectators*. There is, granted, an elitism here, for example, in the often quoted: 'Mankind must work continually at the production of individual great men – that and nothing else is its task' (*UM* III 6). Mankind needs to create favourable conditions for great men to thrive rather like a plant thrives in the right soil. Note the similarity with Plato's views on the need for the right kind of society if the philosopher-king is to flourish. But this should not be interpreted as calling for a society where the elite few bask in glory whilst the many live in the sewers. Nietzsche, rather, is calling for a gradual revolution in which the characteristic of the 'higher' (more adaptive) type become the norm rather than the exception, and so the great individual is not an end in itself – that would be pointless – but rather a means to the redemptive evolution of a whole community. We need leadership, we need role models.

Religion and the state

I have not been asked, as I should have been asked, what the name Zarathustra means in precisely my mouth, in the mouth of the first immoralist ... Zarathustra was the first to see in the struggle between good and evil the actual wheel in the working of things: the translation of morality into the realm of metaphysics, as force, cause, end-in-itself ... Zarathustra created this most fateful of errors, morality: consequently he must also be the first to recognize it ... His teaching, and his alone, upholds truthfulness as the supreme virtue – that is to say, the opposite of the cowardice of the 'idealist', who takes flight in face of reality; Zarathustra has more courage in him than all other thinkers put together.

(*EH*)

The next chapter will consider in some detail Nietzsche's political views (and, indeed, whether Nietzsche *has* any political views) but here it is worth considering the role of religion in any political order proposed by Nietzsche. His views on religion are closely tied with the coming of the Supermen, of the philosophers of the future. These philosophers will possess the virtues of courage, nobility and an ability to face cruel reality rather than hide behind the 'cowardice' of false idealism:

> I deny first a type of man who has hitherto counted as the highest, the good, the benevolent, beneficent; I deny secondly a kind of morality which has come to be accepted and to dominate as morality in itself – decadence morality, in more palpable terms Christian morality.
>
> (*EH*)

Zoroaster is the first prophet to claim that salvation can be obtained through moral behaviour; thus personal responsibility comes to the forefront: one will be judged on the Day of Judgement. Time is perceived as linear, moving morally towards its final consummation in the struggle between good and evil. Nietzsche recognizes the Abrahamic tradition of prophetic religions that appeal to an authority higher than the ancestral or the civil but he would argue that they originate much further back than that: to the work of Zarathustra. This understanding of history is very perceptive; the recognition that Hebrew prophets would have been influenced by Zoroastrian, as well as Greek thought during their period of exile. On many occasions in the notes from the composition of *Zarathustra*, Nietzsche portrays Zarathustra as a lawgiver (*Gesetzgeber*), ranking him alongside Buddha, Moses, Jesus and Muhammad.

Nietzsche, as we shall see in the next chapter, is critical of democracy and the secularization of political authority. As he says in *Human, All Too Human*, 'In the sphere of higher culture there will always have to be sovereign authority, to be sure – but this sovereign authority will hereafter lie in the hands of the *oligarchs of the spirit*.' What is needed to cure social ills 'is not forcible redistribution of property but a gradual transformation of mind: the sense of justice must grow greater in everyone and the instinct for violence weaker.' The capacity to build a new future depends on an ability to see a continuity with the strength of past traditions. An important passage in *Human, All Too Human*, called 'Religion and Government' notes that the importance of religion in the life of a culture is that it consoles the hearts of individuals in times of loss, deprivation and fear; that is, in times when a government is powerless to alleviate the sufferings of people in times of such tragedies as famine and war. However, the increase in democracy has seen a parallel decline in the importance of religion.

Beyond Good and Evil is particularly enlightening when it comes to determining Nietzsche's views on the role of religion. The oligarchs of the spirit in the quote above in *Human, All Too Human* are referred to again in *Beyond Good and Evil*. What is needed, he argues, is a new spiritual aristocracy 'that are strong enough and original enough to give impetus to opposing value judgements and to revalue, to reverse "eternal values"' (*BGE*, 203). Nietzsche's hierarchical society will have a place for religion for it legitimizes the power of rulers and generates obedience as well as providing comfort for the hardship of those who are ruled. Yet Nietzsche of course is not subscribing to Christianity or any other religion of his time, so what would this religion be?

> [...] the one I was just speaking about; and he has come again and again, the god Dionysus, no less, that great ambiguous tempter god, to whom, as you know, I once offered my first-born [*Birth of Tragedy*] in all secrecy and reverence.
>
> (*BGE*, 295)

Dionysus is both life-affirming and satisfies the metaphysical need; a need Nietzsche acknowledges and which is something that modernity cannot offer. All modernity can offer is scepticism, relativism and nihilism.

On Buddhism

Much of Nietzsche's comments on religion were levelled at Christianity, but mention has been made already of Nietzsche's interest in Islam and its culture, and another religion that attracted his curiosity was Buddhism. Like Islam, Nietzsche is much kinder to Buddhism than he is to Christianity, for it lacks what is at the core of Christianity: *ressentiment*.

It should not come as too much of a surprise that Nietzsche talks about Buddhism, as his early enthusiasm for Schopenhauer would have made him aware of the influence of eastern religions on Schopenhauer's philosophy, particularly the emphasis on the eradication of suffering and the world as nothing but illusion. But, like Islam, Nietzsche had a very narrow understanding of Buddhism, seen through the eyes of a select number of German scholars rather than any first-hand experience or the works of Buddhist thinkers from the Eastern tradition. However, no doubt one appeal of Buddhism for Nietzsche is that there is no omnipotent God with the accompanying doctrines on redemption, sin, grace, a separate world, and so on. Consequently, there is no need for prayer or public displays of faith, no need for richly decorated churches and an elitist priestly class:

> Buddhism is a hundred times more realistic than Christianity – it has the heritage of a cool and objective posing of problems in its composition, it arrives *after* a philosophical movement lasting hundreds of years; the concept 'God' is already abolished by the time it arrives. Buddhism is the only really *positivistic* religion history has to show us, even in its epistemology (a strict phenomenalism), it no longer speaks of 'the struggle against sin' but, quite in accordance with actuality, 'the struggle against *suffering*'.

> (*AC*, 20)

The above quote is revealing. It is 'positivistic' in that it is, for Nietzsche, more scientific: that is, it is more in accordance with 'reality'. Rather than emphasize sin, Buddhism focuses on suffering which, again, appealed to Nietzsche for suffering seemed more immediate a condition of human nature than sin. As Buddhists do not have the guilt of sin, they are beyond the hatred and envy that is *ressentiment*. Instead they talk of moderation and benevolence. In addition, because Buddhism has arisen '*after* a philosophical movement lasting hundreds of years' Nietzsche considers it to be a more mature, more *philosophical* religion.

However, Nietzsche still regards Buddhism as a 'decadent' religion and, therefore, no more than one step on the path of nihilism. One key topic that Nietzsche disagreed with is the Buddhist view that suffering stems from desire, and so the only way we can get rid of suffering is through a regimen of mental and physical activities, to get rid of desire. Whilst Nietzsche agrees that suffering is central to human nature and that it is caused by desire, he does not agree that we should therefore get rid of desire, for to do so would be to turn us into inhuman, robot-like, passionless people. What *makes* us human is our suffering. To eliminate desire would not only be wrong and inhuman, but in actual fact impossible if humans are to continue to exist at all.

Summary

- It is inaccurate to say that Nietzsche was, strictly speaking, an 'atheist'. Rather he had a religious point of view, his 'religiosity', although he was very critical of institutionalized Christianity.
- Nietzsche did not escape from his own Lutheran upbringing and can be considered quite traditionalist in many of his views.
- Nietzsche himself had something of a 'religious experience'.
- Nietzsche saw a role for religion, provided it is 'life-enhancing'. This is why he was a strong adherent of Greek culture and religion and would also contrast contemporary Western Christianity with Islam and Buddhism.
- Nietzsche was particularly critical of contemporary modernity and the values that it brings.

09

Nietzsche and politics

In this chapter you will learn:
- about Nietzsche's criticisms of democracy
- what it means to call Nietzsche an 'immoralist'
- about his views on slavery
- about his views on women
- whether Nietzsche actually has any firm political views in his writings.

I am no man, I am dynamite ... It is only beginning with me that the earth knows great politics.

(*EH*, 14:1)

Whilst one important modern debate in academic circles amongst Nietzschean scholars is whether or not he can be considered an ethical naturalist, another fascinating clash of views is on whether or not Nietzsche subscribes to any political views and, if so, what they are.

Democracy

Whilst Nietzsche is a great admirer of Athenian culture, the same cannot be said of that other great Athenian invention: democracy. Rather than support the view held by some, that Athenian culture was a result of democracy, Nietzsche praises the flourishing of the arts in Athens *despite* its democracy, and so sees it more of a hindrance to culture rather than a benefactor. In fact, it seems that Nietzsche's dislike for democracy goes back a long way as he resigned from a student fraternity because he disapproved of what he regarded as a democratic admissions policy. Already, in his student years, we have a man who displayed elitist tendencies even before he had developed any strong philosophic views.

One point that needs to be borne in mind was that at the time Nietzsche was writing, democracy was something of a 'new idea', despite its origins – though in a rather different form than we know it today – in Ancient Greece. Much of Europe at the time was fundamentally aristocratic, and so the view of democracy would have been very different from what, today, is largely taken for granted and considered by many as the best form of government. Having said that, more egalitarian views were certainly being bandied around during his time, not least from his friend Wagner who argued for the abolition of the state and the introduction of radical egalitarianism. In addition, Meysenbug was also a campaigner for democracy and was exiled because of it.

The Birth of Tragedy was originally intended to involve a discussion of politics and it does seem odd that it was omitted. What was to be part of the book became a separate essay called 'The Greek State'. It is an interesting essay and often ignored by scholars, which is a shame as it shows quite clearly that Nietzsche not only had an interest in politics, but was also quite familiar with political theory, perhaps not surprising given the company he kept. The crux of Nietzsche's argument against democracy (as well as feminism, socialism and anarchism) is that it is merely a continuation of Christianity: an ethics of equality that weakens the strong and preserves the failures. He believed that in such a political climate, culture would find it difficult to flourish.

'The Greek State' is a work of cultural criticism, particularly aimed at the contemporary phenomenon of 'modernity' (see previous chapter) with its atomized individualism and such egalitarian themes as the 'dignity of man' and the 'dignity of labour'. The Ancient Greeks, on the other hand, recognized that a life devoted to labour makes it impossible to create great art. Wagner argued that Greek culture cannot be revived because it deserved to perish. Why? Because it was founded upon slavery and so any culturally fulfilled society of the future must exist without slavery, including wage-slavery, characteristic of capitalism which was emerging at the time. Nietzsche, however, in his typically contentious manner, argues that slavery is an essential feature of any society that wishes to attain high culture. Slavery is the essence of culture:

> If culture really rested upon the will of the people, if here inexorable powers did not rule, powers which are law and barrier to the individual, then the contempt for culture, the glorification of 'poorness in spirit', the iconoclastic annihilation of artistic claims would be more than an insurrection of the suppressed masses against drone-like individuals; it would be the cry of compassion tearing down the walls of culture; the desire for justice, for the equalization of suffering, would swamp all other ideas.
>
> ('The Greek State', p.7)

Here Nietzsche is presenting us with a choice: you can have democracy with its smorgasbord of lifestyle options that have no evaluative ranking, thus producing a mood of confusion and cynicism, or you can have aristocracy with its higher states of being, its Superman.

Comparisons can be reasonably made with Plato's conception of the state and those of Nietzsche's. The key difference between Nietzsche and Plato is that for the latter the philosopher-king is one who has access to universal truth, who *discovers* the 'truth', whereas for Nietzsche he is fundamentally, in his early writings anyway, an artist, who *invents* the 'truth'. For Nietzsche it is necessary to recognize that in the modern age, belief in unconditional authority and absolute truth is on the wane. What is distinctive of the modern age is the secularization of political authority: 'In the sphere of higher culture there will always have to be sovereign authority, to be sure – but this sovereign authority will hereafter lie in the hands of the oligarchs of the spirit' (*HAH*, 261). What is needed to cure social ills 'is not forcible redistribution of property but a gradual transformation of mind: the sense of justice must grow greater in everyone and the instinct for violence weaker' (*HAH*, 452). The capacity to build a new future depends on an ability to see a continuity with the strength of past traditions. An important passage in *Human, All Too Human*, called 'Religion and Government' notes that the importance of religion in the life of a culture is that it consoles the hearts of individuals in times of loss, deprivation and fear; that is, in times when a government is powerless to alleviate the sufferings of people during such tragedies as famine and war. However, the increase in democracy has seen a parallel decline in the importance of religion and a greater emphasis on the ego. This, Nietzsche stresses, is not 'individualism' or 'existentialism'.

It is a mistake to interpret Nietzsche, as some scholars such as Derrida do, as someone unconcerned with society or politics, but rather only centred on the asocial, isolated individual. Nietzsche is deeply committed to the promotion of high culture and sees the role of the individual in an Ancient Greek sense as a citizen, as part of a community. His attack on modernity is an attack on liberal democracy with its features of atomistic individuals lost at sea with no values or meaning. In this sense, Nietzsche is very much a traditionalist.

With the decline in political absolutism sanctioned by divine law, there is the possibility that the state, too, will break apart as political authority loses its reverence. Nietzsche hopes that the increase in the secular will lead to a new period of toleration, pluralism and wisdom if chaos and anarchy are to be avoided. Nietzsche, it should be stressed, is not anti-democratic so long as it leaves space for the rare, the unique, and the noble. Democracy does not necessarily lead to the death of high culture and noble values, provided that culture and politics can give each other space. Nietzsche believes that democracy is the political form of the modern world which is best able to offer the best protection of culture; that is, of art, of religion, of all creativity. In his letters he says he is 'speaking of democracy as something yet to come' (293) and favours a social order which 'keeps open all the paths to the accumulation of moderate wealth through work' (285), while preventing 'the sudden or unearned acquisition of riches.'

Nietzsche wishes to preserve a private/public distinction, whereas modern liberal society – although its ideology of the privatization of politics allows individuals a great degree of private freedom – undermines notions of culture and citizenship. Nietzsche's criticisms are levelled against the prevailing democracy of his time, remembering that most of Europe was still autocratic, but was not against a democracy 'yet to come'. This raises interesting debates, occurring in our current time, as to what forms of democracy are possible and a growing awareness that there is not a 'one fits all' political system as has been demonstrated when attempts have been made to impose western forms of democracy on non-western states with devastating consequences. Democratic politics, Nietzsche acknowledges, *can* promote and further culture and, in the recognition that with modernity comes the absence of any possibility of ethical universality, the best hope for the future is that there exists a culture. What kind of 'culture' this would be is uncertain. Would we all agree that Nietzsche's conception of culture, of *high* culture, is one we would accept?

Nietzsche's 'nihilism' is understood in his negative or destructive values, his contempt for values such as democracy, feminism, socialism and so on. These 'modern' ideas Nietzsche sees as lacking in a positive ethos: they are 'slave' values and as such the products of *ressentiment* (see Chapter 04). But it is wrong to accuse Nietzsche of being a nihilist, for a nihilist is only negative and puts nothing forward in its place, whereas Nietzsche is greatly concerned – in fact you could consider it his primary mission throughout much of his life – with a need to present *new* values (even if those 'new' values are a return to ancient values), not simply to get rid of the old ones and put nothing in its place.

As stated above, Nietzsche does resemble Plato in some respects regarding his political views. In fact, *Beyond Good and Evil* contains passages that are remarkably similar: there are the three classes of, first the spiritual leaders, second those who aspire to be leaders and for whom future rulers may arise, and third 'the vast majority who exist to serve and be generally useful and *must* exist only to that end' (Section 61). Like Plato, mention is not specifically made of the 'fourth class', the slaves, but it seems to be a given that slavery would be required 'in one sense or another' (Section 257). Must we then admit that Nietzsche is an advocate of slavery? As stated earlier, Nietzsche was later critical of *The Birth of Tragedy* which he considered a naive and immature work and so it may well be we could forgive his remarks on slavery in 'The Greek State' – written at the same time – as the product of a naive young mind. This cannot be defended, however, as his views remained consistent and, as shown above, he sticks to his guns in his much more mature work *Beyond Good and Evil*. However, it may well be argued that we should not be out to defend or attack Nietzsche, for what he was doing was merely pointing out that culture is, historically speaking, built upon the foundation of cruelty and oppression. If we so choose to create a society that is egalitarian and compassionate then we can say goodbye to high culture and hello to reality TV and celebrity chefs. The debate then centres around whether or not it is the case that liberal society does in fact lead to a recognition that all things have value and, therefore, *nothing* has value. Is twentieth-first century western democracy any less cultural than an aristocratic society would be?

The immoralist?

Leaving aside whether or not a liberal democratic society is capable of achieving such cultural peaks, it is still questionable whether Nietzsche is simply stating what he perceives as a fact or whether he wants to go further and prescribe an aristocratic society with slavery 'in one sense or another'. The fact that Nietzsche considers himself the bringer of an urgent message to mankind makes him come across as the messenger of 'ought' rather than just 'is'. This quote in *The Gay Science* is enlightening:

> ... *virtuous stupidity*; what are needed are unwavering beat-keepers of the *slow* spirit so that the believers of the great common faith stay together and go on dancing their dance; it is an exigency of the first order which commands and demands.

> (*GS*, S76)

There is definitely an 'ought' here; an 'exigency', a necessity, for 'beat-keepers' of 'virtuous stupidity' so that Nietzsche's higher men can 'dance their dance'. Are these 'virtuously stupid' Nietzsche's oppressed slaves who live in misery so that the select few can live in joy? Nietzsche often referred to himself as an 'immoralist' in the sense that he rejected Christian morality, but a number of scholars have gone so far as to say that Nietzsche is, in fact, an immoralist of the highest order; that is, Nietzsche defends views that are morally abhorrent to most people, such as the support of slavery. If such is indeed the case then it brings into serious question why anybody would wish to praise Nietzsche's moral philosophy.

The modern philosopher Julian Young is one who has argued against this understanding of Nietzsche's 'immoralism', stating that a better term to describe Nietzsche's moral outlook is *paternalism*. While paternalism may not be a particularly fashionable view these days, it is in keeping with Nietzsche's time and, indeed, most of human history. This may not help anyone who wants to argue that Nietzsche was ahead of his time, but what this book has hopefully demonstrated, is that Nietzsche was not quite the radical existentialist that he has often been made out to be, but more of a traditionalist who looks *back*, rather than forward. Nietzsche is paternalistic in that he believes most people are *better off* being subordinate and led by stronger figures. Incidentally, as will be considered below, 'most people' was particularly relevant to women. While his views on the 'masses' may be misplaced in relation to modern morality, this does not make him *immoral*, given his concern for the welfare of these 'masses', even if he refers to them mockingly as 'virtuously stupid'!

Other philosophers, notably John Rawls and Philippa Foot, have argued that Nietzsche is not at all concerned with the well-being of the masses and that his only concern is for his Socratic elite. Section 258 of *Beyond Good and Evil* does seem to defend this view:

> When for example an aristocracy like pre-Revolutionary France tosses away its privileges with sublime revulsion and sacrifices itself to its excess of moral feeling, this is corruption: it was really only the final act of that centuries-long corruption that caused the aristocracy to abandon its tyrannical authority bit by bit and reduce itself to a *function* of the monarchy (and ultimately in fact to its ornament and showpiece). The crucial thing about a good and healthy aristocracy, however, is that it does not feel that it is a function (whether of monarchy or community) but rather an *essence* and highest justification – and that therefore it has no misgivings in condoning the sacrifice of a vast number of people who must *for its sake* be oppressed and diminished into incomplete people, slaves, tools.

(*BGE*, 27)

In the same section, Nietzsche goes on to compare society to 'scaffolding' for the greatest to climb. How can this be seen as anything other than a justification for using the masses as 'tools' for the elite? The best defence, again offered by Julian Young, is that Nietzsche does not say here that it is 'my belief', but again is simply stating facts of the past in an anthropological way. What Nietzsche is doing in this section is blaming the French aristocrats for being so complacent and arrogant and 'tossing away' their privileges, thus leading to the collapse of society, to decay and 'corruption'. He is not, in fact, endorsing this particular kind of aristocracy. Nietzsche's more 'spiritual aristocracy' would be of a different kind altogether: one in which the elite would be there for the benefit of society as a whole, not to *use* them for its own ends. This reading can only be understood in the context of other things Nietzsche has said and cannot stand alone, in particular (though by no means exclusively) in *The Antichrist* (see below).

On women

We have seen that one reading of Nietzsche is that his views on slavery are somewhat ambiguous and that it may well be understood as Nietzsche's own anthropological approach to how aristocracies have operated in the past. He then uses this as his model to propose a new state led by a 'spiritual aristocracy' which, being elitist, would no doubt be hierarchical but would be for the benefit of all. This will still leave a bad taste in the mouth of many modern readers brought up in a liberal, egalitarian society, but Nietzsche has given his reasons – whether you agree with him or not – why a liberal, atomized society is actually a lot *worse*.

Comments on women in *Beyond Good and Evil*

A deep man, on the other hand, deep both in spirit and in desire, deep in a benevolence that is capable of rigour and harshness and easily mistaken for them, can think about women only like an *Orient*: he has to conceive of woman as a possession, as securable property, as something predetermined for service and completed in it.

(238)

In no other age have men ever treated the weaker sex with such respect as in our own – it is part of our democratic inclinations and basic taste, as is our irreverence for old age. Is it any wonder that this respect is already being abused? They want more; they are learning to make demands; they end by considering that modicum of respect almost irritating, preferring to compete, or even to battle for their rights: let's just say women are becoming shameless.

(239)

Women want to be autonomous: and to that end they have begun to enlighten men about 'women per se' – *that* is one of the worst signs of progress in Europe's overall *uglification*.

(232)

Stupidity in the kitchen; women as cooks; the frightful thoughtlessness that goes into providing nourishment for families and heads of households! Women don't understand what food *means* – and yet they want to be cooks! If women were sentient beings they would in their thousands of years of cooking experience have discovered the most important physiological facts and taken over the healing art!

(234)

As stated earlier, Nietzsche's 'masses' will seemingly be heavily populated by women, given such comments in *Beyond Good and Evil* (see box). Given such comments it is surprising that articles and books have been written on Nietzsche and feminism! Like his views on slavery, the best we can say perhaps is that this is, again, not Nietzsche being immoral but being paternal or, perhaps more accurately, patriarchal.

However, this still seems unsatisfactory and does not get at a key question here: why, if Nietzsche is actually traditionalist, elitist, aristocrat, anti-egalitarian and sexist, does he appeal so much to modern liberal, free-thinking men *and* women? Whilst part of this appeal may well be due to Nietzsche's unique and 'modern' style, his clever use of metaphor, irony, ambiguity, and so on, it is certainly inadequate to be satisfied with this and simply ignore the actual *content*. Nietzsche, for his part, was out to criticize *European* feminism particularly, in the same way that he attacked just about everything in Europe during his time: nothing escaped his scatter-gun. Feminism was just one of those features of modernity, with its origins in the French Revolution and its ideas of equality. Nietzsche could, and indeed *has*, been conscripted into the feminist cause to some extent by some feminist scholars by emphasizing Nietzsche's attack on equality as an enemy of the Noble spirit: the aristocratic figure, or the philosopher-king if you like. Seen in one context, the 'Noble spirit' can encompass women as well as men in that it is essentially an attack on nineteenth-century egalitarianism that diminishes self-worth rather than women *as such*. However, these may be seen as a somewhat generous reading of Nietzsche.

Jacques Derrida is an important philosopher on Nietzsche, as mentioned in the Introduction. In Derrida's significant work *Spurs*, he comments on the following remark made by Nietzsche in *Beyond Good and Evil*:

Assuming that truth is a woman – what then? Is there not reason to suspect that all philosophers, in so far as they were dogmatists, have known very little about women?

(*BGE*, Preface)

Derrida sees this as arguing that in the same way as there is no single, unitary 'Truth' as such, there is no single, unitary 'woman' *as such*. Nietzsche's criticism of feminism, then, is that it attempts to determine an essence of womanhood, which is doing the same thing as men do to women! That is, women are 'this or that'. In fact, by woman attempting to define herself, she therefore limits her own freedom for ambiguity. Nietzsche's 'Noble spirit' is one that is an artist in the sense that he (or she?) *creates* himself (or herself) and is not limited by any universal essence. It is this understanding of Nietzsche that has its roots in **existentialism**, most succinctly defined by Jean-Paul Sartre as 'existence precedes essence' (see next chapter). Again, however, this seems like a very generous reading of Nietzsche, given the misogynistic quotes above as to what Nietzsche actually says about women in such a deriding manner. It does not seem likely that Nietzsche was talking metaphorically here or, as Derrida suggests, that Nietzsche is actually writing with a 'feminine' voice.

The philosophers of the future

In *Beyond Good and Evil* especially, Nietzsche talks of the 'philosophers of the future' and it has been argued in this chapter that there would be political implications involved (although see below for dispute over this). Nietzsche's comments on these 'leaders' – especially given the German word '*Führer*' – has resulted in many misunderstandings, with visions of blonde Aryan beasts oppressing the masses. It still begs the question, nonetheless, who these philosophers of the future would be and what exactly would they do? Those who would argue against any political agenda at all would see these philosophers as essentially 'free-thinkers', artists, musicians and so on, whereas Nietzsche's use of such terms in *Beyond Good and Evil* as 'commanders and lawgivers' (*BGE*, 211) seems more akin to Plato's philosopher-kings legislating over a new form of society:

I am talking about an increase in the Russian threat so great that Europe would have to decide to become equally threatening, that is, to make use of a new ruling caste in order *to gain a will*, a terrible, long-lived will of its own that could set itself goals over millennia ...

(*BGE*, 208)

Nietzsche's philosopher of the future is not just a codifier of values, but a *creator* of values, a lawgiver, a legislator, and this is why Nietzsche sees such figures of history as Napoleon as a philosopher more than he does, say, Kant. Like Plato's philosopher-kings, Nietzsche's philosophers will be compelled into action, although the temptation to retreat into solitude through disgust with society will be great. In many respects the new philosopher will be like Zarathustra, compelled to 'go down' and encourage people to act. He will be the 'bad conscience' of his age – disagreeing with the majority opinions –and will be derided as such. These new philosophers will also be 'experimenters', not dogmatic in their views. As such, in a Darwinian sense, many will not succeed in their attempts, but it is hoped that years, if not generations, of experimentation will lead to a new age of stability, rather like the Laws of Manu (see below) which Nietzsche also saw as the stable product of many years of empirical experimentation.

Does Nietzsche have any political views?

Some scholars have argued that Nietzsche, in fact, has no political ideals in his writings whatsoever and so to devote a whole chapter to Nietzsche's political views could be misconstrued as way off the mark. However, many other scholars do argue for a 'political Nietzsche' and this chapter is, therefore, quite justified.

As it is hoped has been made clear in this chapter, Nietzsche argued for a hierarchical society – certainly not democratic – in which at the top of the pyramid would be his 'philosophers of the future', his 'oligarchs of the spirit'. This he discusses in *Beyond Good and Evil*, but another very interesting passage can be found in his later work *The Antichrist* in which he praises the Laws of Manu. These laws are Hindu in origin and date back some 2000 years with codes concerning, amongst other things, the caste system. Consequently it is anathema to modern liberals, feminists and so on. No surprise, therefore, that Nietzsche praises it so! He says the following of the Laws of Manu:

> At a certain point in the evolution of a people the most enlightened, that is to say the most reflective and far-sighted class, declares the experience in accordance with which the people is to live – that it *can* live – to be fixed and settled. Their objective is to bring home the richest and completest harvest from the ages of experimentation and *bad* experience. What, consequently, is to be prevented above all is the continuation of experimenting, the perpetuation *ad infinitum* of the fluid condition of values, tests, choices, criticizing of values.

> (*The Antichrist*, S57)

Here Nietzsche is piling praise on a hierarchical system not too dissimilar from Plato's concept of the state ruled by philosopher-kings, and it is no surprise that Nietzsche himself makes this comparison, substituting Plato's philosopher-kings with their mystical vision of the Forms, with his own life-affirming Supermen.

It has been argued that, in the same way Nietzsche seems to praise Islam as a way to contrast it with sickly Christianity, he is doing the same with the Laws of Manu by stating that *even this* is better than Christianity, and Nietzsche was actually quite critical of Manu in his unpublished notes. But, again, we need to ask why he chose not to publish his criticisms and must be wary of remarks he makes in notes that were not intended for public consumption. Rather, Nietzsche sees the Laws of Manu as something of a paradigm: as a model, an empirical attempt, to achieve an ideal, whilst also privately at least acknowledging its flaws. Nietzsche advocates a hierarchical society, but also one much better, more 'natural' than Manu or Plato offer.

Summary

- Nietzsche was, on the whole, critical of democracy as it was beginning to emerge in Europe of his time, although it would be wrong to say that he was against democracy entirely, rather certain forms of democracy.
- His main criticism of democracy was that it can be 'levelling' and so does not allow for great men and great culture to flourish.
- Rather than regard Nietzsche as immoral, perhaps he is better described as 'paternal' in his views on such things as slavery and women.
- Nietzsche's 'philosophers of the future' would not only be artists, musicians and writers but would also be creators of values, legislators and, therefore, political leaders.
- Nietzsche certainly had political views despite the claim by some scholars that he was not concerned with society.

Summary

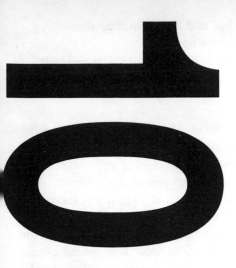

10

Nietzsche's legacy

In this chapter you will learn:
- **the reasons why Nietzsche became associated with Nazism**
- **about the influence Nietzsche had on French twentieth-century philosophy**
- **about his influence on the analytic tradition**
- **about other influences, especially on art and literature.**

Listen to me for I am thus and thus. Do not, above all, confound me with what I am not!

(*EH*, Foreword)

Nazism

It has been said that Nietzsche was in no way a racist, except perhaps towards his own nation, the Germans. Rather, he hated what Germany had become; a nation of people who were nationalists, rather than 'good Europeans' and, worse, who were discriminatory towards others. It is a sad irony, therefore, that he became the official German philosopher. During the World War I, Elisabeth Nietzsche proclaimed her brother as an imperialist and a warrior who would have been proud of the Germans' cause. She arranged for copies of *Thus Spoke Zarathustra* to be sent to the troops.

However, it was with the arrival of the dictators that she was really able to promote Nietzsche's philosophy. She heard that the Italian fascist dictator Mussolini had claimed that Nietzsche was a great influence on him, and so she made a point of establishing a regular correspondence with him. Mussolini took the notion of the Superman to mean anyone who stands out from the crowd and controls his own destiny. In other words, he saw himself in this capacity. Elisabeth praised him as the new Caesar.

When Elisabeth chose to stage a play written by Mussolini at the Archive, the Italian leader was unable to attend. However, the leader of the National Socialist Party, Adolph Hitler, did attend that night. This was her first introduction and she immediately fell under his spell. It was at the Bayreuth Festival on the fiftieth anniversary of Wagner's death that Elisabeth Nietzsche and Adolph Hitler discussed Nietzsche's philosophy. Nietzsche later became the official philosopher of Nazism, giving it the intellectual credibility it otherwise lacked.

Needless to say, after World War II, serious academic study of Nietzsche was neglected as few wished to be associated with the 'Nazi philosopher', yet Nietzsche's own comments on Germans and the German nation may well have resulted in imprisonment or worse during the period of Nazi Germany if they had ever been allowed to be aired in public. Aside from his sister's active encouragement, what other reasons could there be for associating Nietzsche with Hitler?

1. One reason is Nietzsche's association with the Wagners. Richard Wagner himself was an anti-Semite and the Wagners as a whole have been associated with National Socialism. As a consequence any 'disciple' of Wagner is an implied disciple of National Socialism, despite Nietzsche distancing himself from their influence in the late 1870s. As an example, one of the leading figures and theoretical inspirations for Nazi thought was actually an Englishman, Houston Stewart Chamberlain (1855–1927) who became a zealous Germanophile and, significantly, married Richard Wagner's youngest daughter, Eva. Chamberlain wrote an extensive anti-Semitic text called *Foundations of the Nineteenth Century* (1899) which, though a rare thing to find these days, was a bestseller during the rise of Hitler, alongside *Thus Spoke Zarathustra*, and so already these two books were being linked in the German mind.

2. Another reason is that Nietzsche's caustic writing style bears strong similarities to Hitler's, especially in the last two years of Nietzsche's sane life when he became much more rhetorical, combative and violent in tone (see box below). This kind of hatred and venom, though usually in Nietzsche's case an attack on Christians, is not dissimilar from the language used by Hitler to attack the Jews. In *Mein Kampf*, for example, Hitler used terms such as 'parasite' and 'spiritual pestilence'. Nietzsche's 'solution' to such problems, it must be stressed, was largely peaceful in tone, focusing on a revaluation of values, whereas Hitler's 'solution' was far more extreme. Nonetheless, the concern for both was essentially the same in that both strived for a 'healthy' culture and looked to certain sections of humanity that were unhealthy. It was in their methods and focus that they differed drastically.

Nietzsche's violent language

> The priest himself is recognized for what he is: the most dangerous kind of parasite, the actual poison-spider of life.
>
> *(AC,* S38)

> [St Paul was] ... a hate-obsessed false-coiner [counterfeiter].
>
> *(AC,* S42)

> Wherever there is anything small and sick and scabby, there they crawl like lice; and only my disgust stops me from cracking them.
>
> *(TSZ,* Of the Virtue that Makes Small, Part 3.3)

> One does well to put on gloves on reading the New Testament.
>
> *(AC,* 46)

> The ascetic ideal, with its sublime moral cult, with its brilliant and irresponsible use of the emotions for holy purposes, has etched itself on the memory of mankind terribly and unforgettably. I can think of no development that has had a more pernicious effect upon the health of the race, and especially the European race, than this.
>
> *(GM,* Essay 3, Section 21)

3. Another possible reason for Nietzsche's association with National Socialism is that although he was anti-German in many of his remarks, he was a strong believer in community, in the *Volk*. Nietzsche contrasts this form of German romanticism with the seeming emptiness and plurality of modernism; in the poet Hölderlin's (who Nietzsche read voraciously) words, the 'destitution' of modernity. Nietzsche shared the romantic's criticism of modernity, with its emphasis on Enlightenment reason, and stressed instead the importance of community and the role of religion within it (see Chapter 08), but what he distanced himself from was the romantic association with nationalism. *Volkish* thinking became indelibly linked with German nationalism and figures

such as Heinrich Riehl (1823–97), Paul de Lagarde (1827–91) and, importantly, Richard Wagner. Coupled with this German nationalism was anti-Semitism. Despite Nietzsche's own remarks he was associated with these figures.

Twentieth-century French philosophy

> Fundamentally, it is a small number of old Frenchmen to whom I repeatedly return: I believe only in cultivation as it is understood by the French, and hold everything else in Europe that calls itself 'cultivated' to be a misunderstanding, not to mention German culture.

> (*EH*, Why I Am So Clever)

It could reasonably be argued that to understand twentieth-century French philosophy you have to understand Nietzsche. As already stated, Nietzsche hated German nationalism and, to some extent, was not that keen on Germany either. Nietzsche, travelling from one country to another for much of his life, was a true European, and it was French culture especially that he had a soft spot for, despite the fact he spent little time there. Of course, he often spoke admiringly of Muslim countries and culture, yet never spent any time *at all* in a Muslim country.

For its part, France was slow to take on Nietzsche in the philosophy departments, but when it did, it did so by storm. In fact, it was not so much the philosophy departments that took up Nietzsche to begin with, but the country's writers and artists. One such writer, although something of a philosopher, was George Bataille (1897–1962). Under the influence of Nietzsche's views on the Apollonian-Dionysian dichotomy (see Chapter 03), Bataille presented a vision of the world as one that should be Dionysian in character: one in which there is overflowing ecstasy, excess and waste so on. He believed that the production of waste products was a necessity of life and so he would have despaired at modern-day attempts to recycle and create a self-contained equilibrium as an Apollonian, rational monster.

Jean-Paul Sartre (1905–80)

This view of the world as essentially a result of waste products, of a world of dead bodies, flies, dirt, mucus, urine, pus, muggings, phlegm, vomit, dandruff, etc. was the reality portrayed by the existentialist philosopher and writer Jean-Paul Sartre. This world is difficult to face unless we comfort ourselves by creating ideals; illusions in which to cope with the mundane and horrific. The experience of 'nausea' which is described in his novel *Nausea*, is actually a form of enlightenment, an awareness of what it means to be alive. In *Nausea*, the character of Roquentin encounters the world of people and inanimate objects and sees things as having the stamp of his existence upon them. This gives existence a 'nauseating' quality, which is an expression used by Nietzsche in works such as *Thus Spoke Zarathustra* and *Beyond Good and Evil*. Coupled with this concept of nausea is the realization that attempts to deal with objects, situations and people in a rational matter is 'absurd', and this led to a whole school of Absurd literature.

Albert Camus (1913–60)

For the Algerian-born French author, philosopher and journalist Albert Camus, for life to be meaningful we must live every moment like a person who has just come out of prison and smells the fresh air, feels the sunlight and the ground below. This life-affirming attitude is akin to Nietzsche, and Camus considered his thoughts to be a reaction against nihilism. Whilst Camus tried to disassociate himself from any philosophical schools, he was, as a result of his own writings, inevitably linked with existentialism and the Absurd. While Camus never provides a specific doctrine of the Absurd, he nonetheless writes of experiencing the Absurd in, for example the novel *The Stranger* and in his essay *The Myth of Sisyphus*. In this essay, Camus highlights the absurdity of existence by demonstrating that we live a life of paradox: on the one hand valuing our own lives and striving to make something of them, while on the other hand being aware that we are all mortal and so our endeavours will ultimately come to nothing. Camus's interest was not to depress everybody, but rather to consider how we face such absurdity. In fact, he didn't think that life was meaningless: meaning can be created by our own decisions and perspectives, even if this is a temporary thing. This focus on no universals and the death of God – and therefore the death of any kind of absolutes – again was the concern of Nietzsche who likewise rejected nihilism as an option. Camus' intent, *The Fall*, considers the will to power in the context of the weak who, as a final resort, gain a sense of being better than others because they admit they are ridden with guilt.

Henri Bergson (1859–1941)

The Two Sources of Morality and Religion (1932) is the French philosopher Bergson's only published work which mentions Nietzsche by name, but Bergson's philosophy is Nietzschean in many respects. Like Nietzsche, Bergson sets out to reverse Platonism by presenting what has been referred to as process philosophy. That is to say, philosophy does not unravel permanent truths – which would be Platonism – but rather 'truth' is a process involving time, perception, change, memory and intuition. Like Nietzsche's critique of modernity, Bergson attacked mechanistic philosophy of his time, arguing for intelligence as evolutionary and adaptable. Interestingly, Bergson's philosophy had a major influence on the Greek novelist Nikos Kazantzakis (1885–1957) who also read Nietzsche and produced a version of 'process theology', expressed in his major work *Zorba the Greek*. According to Kazantzakis, when we look at the source of religion we see that God is the product of whatever people value.

The influence of Nietzsche on theology is also evident in the writings of Thomas Altizer (b.1927) who helped to create a 'death of God theology' which may strike some as something of an oxymoron, but was nonetheless an attempt to address Nietzsche's concern that Christianity of the time was leading to nihilism. By God's 'death', Altizer is actually referring to the crucifixion of Jesus Christ which, he says, resulted in the pouring out of God's spirit into the world. God's spirit, then, is not transcendent any more, but immanent: it exists in the material world, in the here and now.

Gilles Deleuze (1925–95)

Nietzsche's influence on the French philosopher Deleuze is particularly (though by no means exclusively) evident in his ethics and politics, in that he took up Nietzsche's emphasis on ethical naturalism (see Chapter 04). Like Nietzsche, Deleuze sets out to understand the moral actions and beliefs of people as deriving from their desires and quest for power. To live well is to fully express one's power; that is, to go to the limits of your own potential rather than look for transcendent, universal standards to live by. In *Essays Critical and Clinical,* Deleuze outlines what we must do in the face of a world that is one of flux and difference: 'Herein, perhaps, lies the secret: to bring into existence and not to judge. If it is so disgusting to judge, it is not because everything is of equal value, but on the contrary because what has value can be made or distinguished only by defying judgement. What expert judgement, in art, could ever bear on the work to come?'

Michel Foucault (1926–84)

Perhaps no other French philosopher is more closely associated with Nietzsche than Foucault. Like Nietzsche, he interpreted the world in terms of the will to power and, again, like Nietzsche, had a genealogical agenda which he referred to as 'archaeology': an experimental method which he employed to study aspects of modernity. In the same way an archaeologist literally digs to put together how a society lived, Foucault 'digs' at the form and content of language used in fields of knowledge to reveal the hidden interests of those engaged in discourse, that is, in the dissemination of knowledge. For example, as he states in his work *Discipline and Punish*, when 'experts' (lawyers, psychologists, parole officers and so on) judge on a person's criminality, Foucault sees this as an exercise of power over the criminal. In actual fact, Foucault argues, there is no objective valuation of what a criminal is, and what counts as criminal behaviour in one culture and at one time, can be regarded as legal in another. Like Nietzsche, Foucault attacked Enlightenment attitudes to such concepts as 'inalienable rights', for Foucault would argue that there is no such thing as a universal good. Whilst arguing for no absolutes, Foucault would not allow himself to be drawn into an ethical system or a political agenda, unlike, perhaps, Nietzsche in this respect. Foucault saw it his mission to *investigate*, not to advocate.

The analytic tradition

The **analytic** movement dominated philosophy in Britain and the United States for most of the second half of the twentieth century. Like existentialism, it is difficult to identify specific tenets of this movement, although most analytic philosophers argue that the primary aim of philosophy is, or should be, to look to how language is used. Language, it is argued, is the basis for all our knowledge and so when we use concepts, the important thing is to consider how those concepts are used in the context of language.

It is interesting that whereas existentialism tends to emphasize the irrational and emotional side, the analytic tradition is much more rationalist and logical. Yet Nietzsche succeeds in straddling both traditions. Although Nietzsche is not such a direct influence upon the analytic tradition, much of his philosophy is considered to be firmly within the positivist tradition, particularly his criticism of past philosophers for preoccupying themselves with metaphysical questions and also his view that it is not a matter of 'true' or 'false' but whether a claim makes sense that is important. Further, Nietzsche understood the importance of language in defining our world.

One 'branch' of the analytic movement is called **logical positivism** which adopted a criterion of meaning which stated that unless a statement can be verified by experience (for example, 'all bachelors are happy') or is true by definition (for example, 'a bachelor is an unmarried man') then it is 'meaningless'. This inevitably results in metaphysical statements being discarded as irrelevant to philosophy because such statements like 'God is wise' cannot be proven by experience and nor is it by definition the case that 'God' and 'wisdom' are synonymous (although some have argued that in fact they *are* synonymous).

Art

In literature, Kazantzakis (see page 157) has already been mentioned, as has the fiction of Sartre and Camus. Other writers who have been influenced by Nietzsche and, in fact, have written on Nietzsche, include Thomas Mann (1875–1955), Hermann Hesse (1877–1962), and George Bernard Shaw (1856–1950).

- In the case of Mann, he was particularly interested in Nietzsche's views on the connection between sickness and creativity, which comes across especially in his novel *The Magic Mountain*. Like Nietzsche, Mann argued that disease should not be seen in a wholly negative way, because life and great creativity can come out of illness.
- Hesse's novel *Steppenwolf*, especially, portrays the Nietzschean loner, the 'beast', or 'genius' in the character of Harry Haller who feels out of place in the world of 'everybody'. Hesse lived in Basle for a time, partly because he saw it as the town of Nietzsche.
- Shaw's play *Man and Superman* comes directly from Nietzsche's ideas on the Superman.

Other famous writers influenced by Nietzsche include André Malraux (1901–76), André Gide (1869–1951) and Knut Hamsun (1859–1952), whilst Nietzschean themes crop up amongst the beat poets such as Allen Ginsberg (1926–97) and Gary Snyder (b.1930). Mention should also be made of the Jewish American painter Mark Rothko (1903–70) who was influenced especially by *The Birth of Tragedy*. Rothko saw the mission of art to address the need for modern man to be redeemed from the horrors of life through myth. Rothko regarded himself as a 'mythmaker' as is evident from the titles of so many of his paintings: 'Antigone', 'Oedipus', 'The Sacrifice of Iphigenia', 'The Furies', 'Altar of Orpheus' and so on.

Other influences

The list, quite frankly, is virtually endless. In Russia, the **Symbolists** – who proclaimed art to be the new religion and the Superman to be the artist – adopted Nietzsche's philosophy. Nietzsche's future-orientated philosophy, of man as a 'bridge' to a higher man, influenced revolutionary thinkers such as Trotsky. The psychologist Sigmund Freud (1856–1939) thought highly of Nietzsche, as did Carl Jung (1875–1961). The Austrian psychologist Alfred Adler (1870–1937) founded a school of 'individual psychology' where the emphasis on power dynamics is rooted in the philosophy of Nietzsche. American novelist, philosopher and playwright Ayn Rand (1905–82) was likewise inspired by the writings of Nietzsche.

Nietzsche, no doubt, will continue to influence new generations on a variety of different levels, whether due to his artistic style, the fact that a reader can pick on one profound sentence and write a novel around it, or due to his philosophy specifically which has outlived the man and his age and is as applicable to today's society as it was to Nietzsche's time and the horrors that engulfed Europe in the twentieth century.

Summary

- Nietzsche was against nationalism, especially German nationalism. However, for various reasons, his name became strongly associated with National Socialism.
- Nietzsche was a huge influence on twentieth-century French philosophy especially.
- Nietzsche's stress on the importance of language has affected the analytic tradition.
- Nietzsche was also an influence on a number of painters, dramatists, poets and novelists.

glossary

Amor fati: means to 'love your fate' – a term Nietzsche used to express an affirmation of life.

Analytic: the tradition in philosophy that emphasizes the importance of language in our understanding of the world.

Aphorism: a concise, pithy and often clever saying, varying in length from a single sentence to a short essay of several pages, expressing a general truth.

Correspondence theory of truth: the view that when we talk of things being 'true', then we are referring to things that actually exist in reality. When you point to an object and say 'it is there', then it *really is* there.

Darwinism: a reference to the theories propounded by Charles Darwin (1809–82). Darwin is the founder of modern evolutionary theory.

Dualism: the philosophical position that there are two worlds: the physical and the non-physical.

Empiricism: the philosophical position that we can acquire knowledge of the world through direct experience of the senses.

Existentialism: the philosophical movement that emphasizes human freedom.

Idealism: stresses the importance of the mind in understanding what we can know about the world. At the most extreme, it argues that there is only the mind and no external world.

Logical positivism: an expression of the analytic tradition in philosophy; argued that statements are meaningless if they cannot be verified.

Metaphysics: the speculation on what exists beyond the physical world, such as the existence of God, what is real, and so on.

Modernity: a term with many meanings, but generally a reference to the increase in secularization accompanied by a belief in scientific progress.

Monism: the view that ultimately reality is composed of only one substance. It is, therefore, opposed to dualism.

Nihilism: literally a 'belief in nothing' although there are varying levels of nihilism. At the less extreme it is a rejection of contemporary values and traditions, but does present the possibility of alternatives.

Noumena: metaphysical beliefs about the soul, the cosmos, and God which are matters of faith rather than of scientific knowledge.

Orientalist: a term used to describe western writings and writers who present a romantic and distorted picture of the east, or the 'Orient'.

Pantheism: the belief that there are not two worlds, but one and this is identified with God.

Perspectivism: the view that we perceive the world according to our perspective, although this may not be as the world actually is.

Phenomena: in Kantian terms, the world of everyday things that we can detect with our senses.

Philology: the study of language and literature.

Pragmatic theory of truth: the opposite of the 'correspondence theory of truth'. Something is only 'true' to the extent that it is practical to believe in it.

Rationalism: the philosophical position that reason, the intellect, forms the basis for much of our knowledge.

Relativism: morals and beliefs are a product of a particular time and place and, therefore, there is no such thing as 'right' and 'wrong'.

Ressentiment: the French word for resentment. Nietzsche uses it to explain his genealogy of morals. *Ressentiment* is the hostility that the slave feels towards the master.

Timeline of important events in Nietzsche's life

1844	Friedrich Wilhelm Nietzsche born on 15 October in Röcken, a small village near Lützen.
1849	Death of Nietzsche's father on 30 July, diagnosed as softening of the brain.
1850	Nietzsche's brother, Ludwig Joseph, dies on 9 January. The family relocates to Naumburg in early April.
1856	Nietzsche writes his first philosophical essay, 'On the Origin of Evil'.
1858	In October he is accepted into the Pforta School.
1862	Together with a few friends, he founds the literary club 'Germania'.
1864	In October he begins studying theological and classical philology in Bonn.
1865	Leaves Bonn and moves to Leipzig to study philology. He has given up on theology. In October he discovers Schopenhauer.
1868	Becomes friends with Wagner.
1869	Appointed to the University of Basel.
1870	Military service as a medic. He falls ill with dysentery and diphtheria.
1872	*The Birth of Tragedy* is published. It is rejected by scholars.

1876	Becomes friends with Rée and attends the first Bayreuth Festival. He makes his mind up to break with Wagner.
1879	Resigns from his university teaching and starts his nomadic life.
1881	His first visit to Sils-Maria. Has his great 'inspiration' and writes of eternal recurrence.
1882	Proposes marriage to Lou Salomé twice.
1883	Death of Wagner on 13 February.
1885	Nietzsche's sister marries Bernhard Förster in May.
1889	Nietzsche breaks down and never recovers from mental illness.
1900	Dies on 25 August.

Chronology of major works

Birth of Tragedy (BT)	1871
Untimely Meditations (UM) 1	1873
2, 3	1874
4	1876
Human, All Too Human (HAH)	1878
The Wanderer and His Shadow	1880
Dawn (WSD)	1881
The Gay Science (GS)	1882
Thus Spoke Zarathustra 1, 2 *(TSZ)*	1883
	1884
	1885
Beyond Good and Evil (BGE)	1886
The Genealogy of Morals (GM)	1887
The Twilight of the Idols (TI)	1889
The Antichrist (AC)	
	1889
Ecce Homo (EH)	1889
Nietzsche contra Wagner (NW)	1889

Further reading

Books written by Nietzsche:

For dipping into you might like to pick up a copy of *A Nietzsche Reader* (Penguin) edited and translated by R. J. Hollingdale, which divides Nietzsche's writings into themes. Another good read is *The Portable Nietzsche* (Viking Penguin) edited and translated by Walter Kaufmann. This includes sections from Nietzsche's works, as well as his notes and letters.

Here is a selection of Nietzsche's works:

Beyond Good and Evil, translated by R. J. Hollingdale, Penguin. The translation by Marion Faber (Oxford Paperbacks) is also very good.

Thus Spoke Zarathustra, translated by R. J. Hollingdale, Penguin.

Twilight of the Idols, translated by R. J. Hollingdale, Penguin.

Human All Too Human, translated by Marion Faber, Penguin.

The Birth of Tragedy, translated by Shaun Whiteside, Penguin.

Ecce Homo, translated by R. J. Hollingdale, Penguin

Books about Nietzsche and his work:

The following are good general introductions to Nietzsche's life and work:

Chamberlain, L. (1997) *Nietzsche in Turin*, Quartet Books. (This presents a portrait of Nietzsche in the last year of his sane life.)

Hollingdale, R. J. (2001) *Nietzsche: The Man and His Philosophy*, CUP

Stern, J. P. (1978) *Nietzsche*, Fontana

Tanner, M. (2000) *Nietzsche*, OUP

Wicks, R. (2002) *Nietzsche*, One World

The following are more detailed commentaries on Nietzsche's work:

Ansell-Pearson, K. (1994) *An Introduction to Nietzsche as Political Thinker*, CUP (Argues that Nietzsche does have a political philosophy.)

Burnham, D. (2006) *Reading Nietzsche: An Analysis of Beyond Good and Evil*, Acumen Publishing (Another good section-by-section commentary on *Beyond Good and Evil*.)

Lampert, L. (2004) *Nietzsche's Task*, Yale University Press (A section-by-section commentary on *Beyond Good and Evil*.)

Lampert, L. (1989) *Nietzsche's Teaching*, Yale University Press. (An interpretation of *Thus Spoke Zarathustra*.)

Leiter, B. (2002) *Nietzsche on Morality*, Routledge. (Brian is an analytic philosopher and argues for Nietzsche's ethical naturalism.)

Safranski, R. (2003) *Nietzsche: A Philosophical Biography*, Granta (An interesting mix of biography with Nietzsche's philosophy.)

Welshon, R. (2004) *The Philosophy of Nietzsche*, McGill-Queen's University Press (A detailed look at the key themes of Nietzsche's teaching.)

Websites

The Nietzsche Circle (**http://nietzschecircle.com/**) describes itself as an 'artistic and intellectual community' that explores Nietzsche's philosophy.

Brian Leiter's Nietzsche blog (**http://brianleiternietzsche.blogspot.com/**) has some interesting material.

Friedrich Nietzsche Society (**http://www.fns.org.uk/**) was founded in 1990. It organizes an annual conference.

index

Page numbers in **bold** are for glossary entries, e.g. Darwinism 84, **163**
Books and essays listed in the index are by Nietzsche unless indicated otherwise.

Absurd, school of 156–7
Adler, Alfred 161
aestheticism 47
affirmation, of life 98, 103, 121, 123
Altizer, Thomas 157–8
amor fati 103, **163**
analytic tradition xvii, 159–60, **163**
ancient Greeks *see* Greece, ancient
The Anti-Christ 32, 73, 85, 111, 127, 148
anti-Semitism 10, 12, 33–4, 65, 153
aphorism(s) xiv–xv, 23, **163**
Apollonian principle 43, 45
Apollonian–Dionysian dualism 42–4, 45, 97, 155
Aristotle 56
Art, life as 48–50, 97, 104
  Nietzsche's influence on 160–1
Art–Nature dualism 42–3, 155
atheism 120–1
Athenian culture *see* Greece, ancient

Bataille, Georges 155
Bayreuth Festival (1876) 12–13, 33
belief 55–6, 111, 114
Bentham, Jeremy 56–7
Bergson, Henri 157–8
Berkley, George 15–16
Beyond Good and Evil 24–5
  on democracy and class 140
  how to read it xiv
  and metaphysical speculation 77–8
  and moral values 55, 57–8, 59, 62
  and nihilism 100–1
  the 'philosophers of the future' 146–7
  and religion 131
  and Will to Power 74, 76, 84
Birth of Tragedy 8, 12, 38–51, 140
  the Apollonian–Dionysian dualism 42–4, 45, 97, 155

and culture 45–8
and redemption 93
the 'theoretical man' 39–42
and value of Greek tragedy 48–50
and Will to Power 82
Buddhism 19, 101, 132–3
Burckhardt, Jakob 8, 45, 46–7

Camus, Albert 156–7
causation 16, 115
cave allegory (Plato) 82–3
chorus, in Greek tragedy 45–6, 48
Christianity
  compared with other religions 125, 132, 148
  Lutheran tradition 2–3, 35, 122–3
  morality of 56, 62–7, 68
  view of afterlife 95
  see also God; religion
class *see* elitism; hierarchical society; social class
'common sense' 112, 115–16
compassion/pity 63, 68, 124–5
consciousness 18
correspondence theory 102–3, 109–10, **163**
'cosmological' view 84
culture 45–8, 128–9
  and democracy 137–41
  high culture 130, 138–9, 140, 141

Darwinism 84, **163**
Dawn 24
Daybreak 23, 26–7
deconstruction 47–8
deduction 60
Deleuze, Gilles 158
democracy 136–41
Derrida, Jacques 145–6
Descartes, Rene 15, 84–5

Dionysian principle 43–4, 45–6, 48–9, 97, 131, 155
Dithyrambs of Dionysus 32
dreams *see* illusion(s)
dualism 15, **163**

Ecce Homo 27–8, 32, 61–3, 123
elitism/the elite 67, 129, 130, 142–3
empiricism 15, 83–6, **163**
energy, time and infinity 96–7
enhancement 82, 124–5
epistemology 108
Eternal Recurrence 27–8, 94–8, 99, 103
ethical naturalism 56–61
Euripedes 48
European nihilism 101–2
existence, nature of 14–15
existentialism 57, 146, 156, **163**
extended substance (matter) 15

factual statements 60–1
feminism 145–6
Förster, Bernhard (brother-in-law) 33–4
Förster-Nietzsche, Elisabeth (sister) 3, 30, 31, 33–5
    nationalist/anti-Semitic ideology 65–6, 76, 99, 152
    publication of Nietzsche's work xiv, 35, 76, 95–6, 148
Foucault, Michel 56, 57, 158–9
Franco-Prussian War 7, 46
Fraser, Giles 120–1
French philosophy xvii, 155–9
Freud, Sigmund 56, 161

Gast, Peter 25–6, 28, 29
The Gay Science 24, 56, 90, 94, 98, 141
The Genealogy of Morals 55, 59, 61
German nationalism 10, 12, 65, 99, 152
Gersdorff, Carl von 26
God
    Buddhist non-belief in 132
    death of ('God is dead') xi, 55–6, 67, 91, 121
    see also Christianity; religion
'good', and 'bad' or 'evil' 64, 66, 90
Greece, ancient
    democracy and culture 136, 137
    philosophy 14, 56, 75, 95
    tragedy 38, 39, 45–6, 48–50
'The Greek State' 46–7, 137–8, 140

'health' 123, 125
    see also suffering
Heidegger, Martin 120
Heine, Heinrich 95
Heller, Erich 120
herd morality 66, 67, 128
Hesse, Hermann 160
hierarchical society 131, 147–9
high culture 130, 138–9, 140, 141
Hinduism 148

history
    and illusion 47–8
    monumental 128–9
Human, All Too Human 9, 23, 112–13, 130–1, 138
Hume, David 16–17, 59–60, 115

idealism 16, **163**
ideas
    and impressions 16
    of sensation and reflection 15–16
    and Will 18
illusion(s) 43, 45, 47–8, 112–13
'immoralism' 141–3
impressions, and ideas 16
infinity, time and energy 96–7
'inspiration' 27–8, 123–4
instinct 122
intoxication 43–4
Islam 125–7

Jesus 66–7, 128, 158

Kant, Immanuel 16–17, 50, 56, 57, 111
Kazantzakis, Nikos 157
knowledge, theory of 108
Krug, Gustav 3, 4

Lange, F. A. 6
language xvii, 76–7, 114–17, 153, 154
Laws of Manu 148–9
leadership *see* elitism; hierarchical society; 'philosophers of the future'; 'spiritual aristocracy'; Superman
life
    affirmation of 98, 103, 121, 123
    and 'afterlife' 95, 96–8, 99
    as Art 48–50, 97, 104
    see also amor fati; enhancement
literature
    Nietzsche's influence on 160
    Nietzsche's musical/literary interests xv, 5, 9, 38, 41, 49–50
Locke, Jon 15–16
logical positivism 159–60, **164**
Lutheran tradition 2–3, 35, 122–3

Mann, Thomas 160
Manu, Laws of 148–9
marriage 24, 29, 30
the 'masses' 67, 141–3
material monism 75
meaning, and Will to Power 82
meta-ethics 54–5
metaphysics 40, 77, **164**
Meysenbug, Malwida von 22–4, 136
modernity 47, 127–8, 131, 154, **164**
monism 75, **164**
monumental history 128–9
morality 54–5
    and death of God 56
    and early Christianity 66–7

'immoralism' 141–3
slave morality 61–6
see also Christianity; religion; values
motive, and morality 61–2, 64–5
music xv, 5, 41, 49–50
Mussolini, Benito 152
myth 128

nationalism 10, 12, 65, 99, 152
naturalism, ethical 56–61
naturalistic fallacy 59–60
nausea 156
Nazism 35, 65, 99, 152–5
New Germany 34
Nietzsche contra Wagner 32
Nietzsche, Elisabeth *see* Förster-
Nietzsche, Elisabeth
Nietzsche, Franziska (mother) 2, 3, 4, 33
Nietzsche, Friedrich Wilhelm
academic career 5–9
biography of 35
character of 4–5, 68
elitist tendencies 136
love of solitude 25, 100
death and funeral 35
early life and education xv–xvi, 2–6, 9,
122
friendships 4, 22–3, 25–6, 28–9, 30–1
Wagner 6, 9–11, 23, 38, 50
illnesses xii, 5, 6, 8, 24, 68, 100
insanity xvi–xvii, 32–3, 34
language use xvii, 76–7, 114–17, 153,
154
life in Italy and France 22–3, 25–6,
28–32, 100
marriage and sexuality 30
musical/literary interests xv, 5, 9, 38,
41, 49–50
notes published by sister xiv, 35, 76,
95–6, 148
as philologist 5, 98
physical appearance 7–8
published work attacked 38
spiritual experience 27–8, 123–4
university and academic career 6–9
wanderings 24–8
writing style xiii–xv, 79, 100, 116,
153–4
Nietzsche, Karl Ludwig (father) 2, 3, 4
Nietzsche Archive 34–5
nihilism 100–3, 122–3, 140, **164**
'Noble spirit 145
normative ethics 54–5
noumena 17–18, 104, **164**

objective values
human need for 104–5
Will to Power as objective explanation
72, 75–8
see also rationalism; reason; truth;
values
Of Self-Overcoming 92

'On Truth and Lie in a Morally-Disengaged
Sense' 111, 114–15
Oriental nihilism 100
orientalism/orientalist 125–6, **164**
Origin of Moral Sensations 23
the Other 125–6

pantheism 15, **164**
paternalism 142
Paul, St. 66, 67
perspectivism 110–13, **164**
phenomena 17–18, **164**
philology 5, 98, **164**
philosopher king 129, 138, 145, 148
see also elitism; high culture
'philosophers of the future' 130, 146–7
philosophy *see* analytic tradition; French
philosophy; Greece, ancient
pietism 122
Pinder, Wilhelm 4
pity/compassion 63, 68, 124–5
Plato 14–15, 40, 82–3, 113, 138, 148
politics 136–49
and democracy 136–41
and 'immoralism' 141–3
Nietzsche's views on 147–9
the 'philosophers of the future' 146–7
religion, and the state 129–31
and women 143–6
power, and morality 63–5
pragmatic theory of truth **164**
priesthood, Christian 66–7
private/public dualism 139
'process theology' 157
psychology 161
public/private dualism 139
Pythagoras 95

rationalism 15, 40–1, 48–9, 57, 113, **164**
the reader xiv, 80
'real world' 116–17
see also 'common sense'; noumena;
senses; truth
reason 40–1, 49, 50, 113–14
redemption 93, 123
Rée, Paul 22, 23, 29, 90, 125
relativism 40–1, **164**
religion 120–33
culture and democracy 138
experience of as 'inspiration' 27–8,
123–4
and illusion 47–8
as life-enhancing 124–5
Lutheran tradition 2–3, 35, 122–3
and morality 56, 62–3, 68
Nietzsche's religiosity 120–1
and the state 129–31
and theology 157–8
see also Buddhism; Christianity;
God; Hinduism; Islam;
Zoroastrianism
ressentiment 64–5, 132, 133, **165**

Roman empire, and Christian values 63, 65–7
romanticism 154
Rothko, Mark 160–1
Russell, Bertrand 114
Russian Symbolists 161

Salomé, Lou von 28–31, 90
salvation 102, 103, 121, 123
Sartre, Jean-Paul 146, 156
Schopenhauer, Arthur 17–19
  and Buddhism 19, 101, 132
  and Eternal Recurrence 95
  influence on Nietzsche 6, 14, 19, 50
  nihilism of 101
  and religion 125, 133
  Will 18, 19, 44, 63, 77
scientific methods 48, 58–9, 83–4, 104–5
  see also empiricism
the self, and Will to Power 81–2, 84–5
the senses, and reason 113–14
Shaw, G. B. S. 160
Simmel, Georg 97
slave morality 61–6
slavery 137, 140, 141
social class 66, 67, 140
society
  and democracy 137–41
  hierarchical system of 131, 147–9
  and the 'masses' 67, 141–3
  see also democracy; elitism;
    'philosophers of the future'; 'spiritual
    aristocracy'; Superman
Socrates 40–1, 49, 83
solitude 25, 90–1, 100
Spinoza, Baruch 15
'spiritual aristocracy' 130–1, 138, 140,
  143
spiritual experiences 27–8, 123–4
the state
  and culture 138–9
  and religion 129–31
'states of energy' 96, 97
Strauss, David 47–8
subjective explanation, Will to Power as
  72, 79–83
suffering (pain) 123, 132–3
Superman 67–8, 91, 98–9, 103
Symbolists 161

Thales 75
theology 5, 157–8
thinking substance (soul) 15
Thus Spoke Zarathustra 24, 28, 31, 90–3
  the Eternal Recurrence 94–8
  'inspiration' for 123
  Nietzsche's philosophy after Zarathustra
    100
  sent to German troops 152
  the Superman 98–9
  and Will to Power 77, 81, 82–3

time, energy and infinity 96–7
truth
  and Art 49
  and belief 55, 111
  concepts of 82–3, 114–15, 138
  correspondence theory of 102–3,
    109–10, **163**
  and subjective interpretation 79–81
  varieties of 108–9
  see also morality; values
Turgenev, Ivan 101–2
The Twilight of the Idols 32, 78, 113, 114,
  121

Übermensch see Superman
Untimely Meditations 13, 47–8, 95
utilitarianism 56–7, 60–1, 62

value statements 60–1
values
  and beliefs (death of God) xi, 55–6, 67
  compassion and pity 63, 68, 124–5
  ethical naturalism 56–61
  human need for objective 104–5
  lacking in Will to Power 85–6
  nihilist view of 102–3, 140
  and the 'Superman' 67–8
  see also aestheticism; morality; truth
Volk 11, 128, 154–5

Wagner, Richard 9–13
  anti-Semitism of 33–4, 65, 153
  egalitarian views 136
  Nietzsche's association with 6, 23,
    38–9, 50
The Wagner Case 32
war, and culture 46–7
Weimar 35
Will
  as 'drives' 85
  Schopenhauer on 18, 19, 44, 63, 77
Will to Power 19, 63, 72–87
  concept of 72–4
  as empirically true 83–6
  as objective explanation 72, 75–8
  as subjective explanation 72, 79–83
Will to Power (Förster-Nietzsche) 35, 73,
  74, 76
women 4, 143–6
writers, Nietzsche's influence on 160

Zarathustra, story of 25, 27, 28, 90–3,
  129, 130
  see also Thus Spoke Zarathustra
Zoroastrianism 90, 130